PRAISE FOR
MONEY SHACKLES

"Dutch's provocative encouragement of the pursuit of alternative investment strategies is a refreshing departure from conventional portfolio management approaches. He reveals opportunities for the everyman investor and nails it."

—ETAN BUTLER, Chairman, Dalmore Group

"As someone who's spent decades in the alternative investment space, Dutch explains every nook and cranny your average investor isn't taking advantage of… or even aware of."

—TAYLOR AND MEGAN KOVAR, Founders of
Kovar Wealth Management, The Money Couple

"Dutch is redefining the American Dream for the modern age. He leads from his heart with grace, humility, and dignity. I am proud to have witnessed all he's come to accomplish over the years. It is wonderful to see him sharing his lessons and learnings, his hardships, and wins to empower others to break their status quo and challenge what defines financial freedom. Breaking out of your comfort zone and challenging yourself is when you grow to build a better version of you and find out what you are capable of achieving - Dutch is the model of this and challenges others to find their meaning of financial freedom."

—REBECCA KACABA, CEO and Co-Founder, Dealmaker

T0036970

MONEY SHACKLES

The Breakout Guide
to Alternative Investing

DUTCH MENDENHALL

Copyright © Dutch Mendenhall 2021. All Rights Reserved.
ISBN paperback: 9781954759282
ISBN hardcover: 9781954759299
ISBN ebook: 9781954759275
Published by Michaels Press
Distributed by National Book Network

All rights reserved. No part of this publication may be reproduced,
stored in a retrieval system, or transmitted in any form or by
any means, electronic, mechanical, photocopying, recording or
otherwise without the prior written permission of the publisher.

Printed in the United States of America.

For more information call 702-216-2995
or visit https://michaelspress.com/

THE BREAKOUT GUIDE TO ALTERNATIVE INVESTING

This book exposes many Americans' harsh reality of financial vulnerability.

Examining the societal pressures that can lead to debt provides insights to help you move toward financial freedom, regardless of your current financial standing.

You will explore how to control your financial future by understanding your money personality, the concept of diversification, and specific alternative investing methods like Fractional Ownership. The book empowers you by providing actionable strategies for alternative investments and other proven tactics for attaining financial freedom.

CONTENTS

SPECIAL ACKNOWLEDGMENTS

First and foremost, thank you to my wonderfully intelligent and beautiful wife, **Vanessa Mendenhall.** Thank you for being the constant source of love and support in my life and the foundation on which we have built our lives together. Without you, I could not have achieved all that I have.

Thank you, **Amy Vaughn**, for being the driving force behind our shared vision, the best business partner and fellow co-founder anyone can hope to have, and for bringing their unique talents and perspective to every challenge we face. Your hard work, dedication, and expertise have been instrumental in our success, and I am forever grateful for your partnership.

Thank you, my brilliant niece, **Anna Mendenhall**, for her work on this book and for bringing her unique talent and perspective to every page. Your dedication, skill, and creativity have been nothing short of remarkable.

Where would I be today without my brothers? Thank you, **Randy**, **Brent**, and **Dory Mendenhall**, for your love and support, especially Dory's extraordinary role in my life. From raising me and introducing me to new opportunities, you gave me the freedom to focus on our impact and pursue my passions, and I am forever grateful for your guidance and support.

I would also like to extend my deepest gratitude to some talented team members from my RAD Diversified[1] family, who have been the best in helping create this book. **Leonard Mello**, **Erin Hyde**, **Zach Sprague**, **Nate Hernandez**, **Chris Fuentes**, and **Jacob Barriga**. What can I say, I love this amazing team. Their unwavering support, artistic and creative input or insightful editorial feedback, and tireless dedication have been invaluable throughout the writing process. This book wouldn't be completed without you. Thank you for being a part of this journey with me.

Thank you, **Corinthia Davis**, **Sarita Lee**, **Kevin Mantell**, **Jeff Thomas**, **Robin Thomas**, and **Eric Snell,** who graciously shared their stories and experiences for this book. Your willingness to open up and share your journeys has been inspiring and humbling. Thank you for trusting me with your stories.

Thank you, **Ron Eccles**, for being a friend and fellow walker in faith. He is an accomplished success coach for entrepreneurs[2] and an educator at RAD Diversified, who has developed many of the concepts that have contributed to this book. It stands to reason Ron's expertise went to helping and making a few suggestions in the chapters and exercises to be engaging and effective for readers to achieve their goals.

Thank you, **Natallia Filatova**, for illustrating this book.[3] Your talent has transformed the text into visual aid masterpieces, and it's been great to collaborate with such an artist.

---

1   n/d. 2019 (2023). *RAD Diversified: Real Estate Investment Trusts.* Retrieved from https://raddiversified.com/.

2   n/d. 2010 (2023). *Dr. Ron Eccles.* Retrieved from https://drroneccles.com/.

3   n/d. 2018 (2023). *ipamia.* Retrieved from https://www.fiverr.com/ipamia (https://www.instagram.com/ipamia.art/).

Thank you, **The Money Couple**[4], who contributed to Chapter 3, helping shape my financial beliefs and guiding me in communicating these ideas to my readers. Their dedication to assisting others in achieving financial harmony is genuinely inspiring.

Thank you, **Etan Butler**, Chairman of Dalmore Group.[5] Your guidance helped gather the resources needed for Chapter 6. His efforts contributed to the chapter's depth and accuracy.

Thank you, **Rebecca Kacaba**, the CEO and Co-Founder of Dealmaker,[6] whose thoughtful feedback and suggestions greatly improved Chapter 7. Her keen eyes helped refine and clarify my ideas, resulting in a more substantial and impactful chapter.

Thank you, **Nate Goad**, the Florida Market President and Consultant with Alden Investment Group,[7] whose expertise was essential to developing Chapter 9. His knowledge and willingness to share his perspectives helped shape the chapter into a more prosperous journey for the reader.

Thank you, **Michael Drew**, **Anthony Garcia**, and **Robert Hughes** at Promote a Book,[8] for their contributions to the writing of this book. Their feedback and support have been instrumental in making this book possible.

Finally, I want to thank my friends and family, who I may not have mentioned by name but have provided encouragement, support, and

---

4   n/d. 2002; 2020 (2023). *Marriage and Financial Advice to Couples: The Money Couple.* Retrieved from https://themoneycouple.com/.

5   n/d. 2019 (2023). *Dalmore Group: Leading Broker-Dealer for Reg A+.* Retrieved from https://dalmorefg.com/.

6   n/d. 2018 (2023). *DealMaker: Equity Crowdfunding Technology.* Retrieved from https://www.dealmaker.tech/.

7   n/d. 1995 (2023). *Broker/Dealer & Registered Investment Advisor.* Alden Investment Group. Retrieved from https://aldeninvestmentgroup.com/.

8   n/d. 2009 (2023). *Promote A Book.* Retrieved from https://promoteabook.com/.

inspiration throughout the writing process. Your unwavering belief in me and my work gave me the motivation and confidence to see this project through to completion.

CHAPTER 1

THE REALITY OF FINANCIAL VULNERABILITY

Have you been sold someone else's American Dream?

She was called the Moses of her people.[9]

Harriet Tubman.

Her story is about breaking the shackles to freedom.

Born into slavery. Abused, tormented, deprived, and dehumanized. Resilient.

What American doesn't know about her?

Harriet Tubman was more than an abolitionist and great orator. More than a scout, spy, nurse, or cook. More than a conductor, suffragist, caretaker, or even humanitarian. She still represents a beacon of freedom and hope that resonates with all generations.

She overcame an oppressive economic system of slavery that perpetuated the power and wealth of the classes. Her circumstances didn't define

---

9   Bradford, SH. 1886 (2006). *Harriet Tubman: The Moses of Her People*. Retrieved from https://www.gutenberg.org/ebooks/9999.

her. Her life was always at risk to help hundreds, challenging the status quo and continuing to speak out against economic and social systems that marginalized and oppressed individuals in her later life.

She wasn't someone to sit by and watch. She took massive action.

Harriet Tubman is a woman of unwavering determination, a testament to the human spirit and how the power of collective action can create a more equitable society.

From shackles to freedom: her story liberated millions.

"I want to change the game. I want to change the system. This book is about my journey from shackles to freedom."—Dutch Mendenhall

"This can't be my life. This isn't my life," I told myself.

Sitting outside a restaurant on a cold New Year's night, that was never more true. My life sucked. I was working as a valet, and people were walking by. Many didn't even bother tipping. It was as if I didn't exist.

"I had a distinct sense of emptiness that something was missing. I realized every decision, every action, and every situation I ran into impacted my life."

I had a distinct sense of emptiness that something was missing. I realized every decision, every action, and every situation I ran into impacted my life.

I felt like I was a ghost of who I was supposed to be, and at that moment, the direction of my life changed.

What if my life could be different?

I believe that even though some events were beyond my control, I still had the ability to actively steer my life in the direction I wanted. I realized I had the power to create the path.

I was feeling more detached from my life and my identity. I was feeling more like a spectator than a participant. I had transformed into a spectral-like figure who was empty and cold. I felt overburdened and underwhelmed by aspirations and dreams for the future.

I took the time to write down where I was in life. I put pen to paper to assess who I was that day.

Then I took the time to write down who I knew I was meant to be, the story of my future—my **Redefined American Dream**, not the one being sold to me—and what I wanted out of life. What I wrote down was not who I was supposed to be. It was not who those around me said I should be. Not what society said I should be. Not what the rest of the world said I should be.

I wrote down who I knew I was meant to be and what I wanted to achieve. I knew I had to break free of the "Money Shackles" on me and the "Freedom Trap" I was in, without control of my fate.

Have you felt this? Even briefly? So impacted by feeling empty or disconnected from life. Have you analyzed what's causing some of those feelings? In 2005, I could see what was holding me back clearly—I was bound by my "Money Shackles" and financial obligations that could limit my financial freedom. The chains of habit are too light to be felt until they are too heavy to be broken. Breaking free from "Money Shackles" requires taking control of your financial situation, making smart alternative decisions, making money and debt work for you, and investing in your future. Today, if you haven't felt the sting of supply-chain issues, inflation, and the stress of money, you've been living under a rock on the moon. According to the American Psychological Association, over 80% of Americans worry about how the supply chains will affect their daily lives and needs and feel inflation's stress.[10] Over 60% say money is the source of all of their stress.

---

10 *Stress in America. 2022. Money, inflation, war pile on to nation stuck in COVID-19 survival mode.* Retrieved from https://www.apa.org/news/press/releases/stress/2022/march-2022-survival-mode.

These very real stressors are "Money Shackles." We could dive into what is causing current events, but ultimately they define and control everyday Americans' livelihoods. They are part of creating systematic processes in America that don't allow people to break out to financial freedom to live their American Dream.

What is the American Dream to you?

"We hold these truths to be self-evident, that all men are created equal, that they are endowed by their Creator with certain unalienable Rights, that among these are Life, Liberty and the pursuit of Happiness."

—The Declaration of Independence[11]

In America, individual empowerment and ownership are essential to achieving the American Dream—a belief I have internalized throughout

---

11   Jefferson, T, et al. 1776. *The Declaration of Independence*. Retrieved from https://www.archives.gov/founding-docs/declaration-transcript

my life. The American Dream started with the revolutionary idea of breaking free from colonial governance and controlling our destiny. The American people were tired of being subjected to the tyranny of class taxation and fought for the freedom to pursue their interests and futures.

Guided by a culture of openness, a spirit of adventure, entrepreneurship, freedom of movement, religious liberty, and hard work, Americans had the opportunity to prosper and create a better life for themselves and their children by capitalizing on opportunities and hard work. Our freedom has been instrumental in this journey, providing the platform for success and the means to secure a brighter future for future generations.

People still want the traditional American Dream but face a difficult economic reality today.

The American Dream has evolved to encompass more than political freedom since the colonial revolution era, when the traditional version of the American Dream centered on individual ownership and self-sufficiency. The influx of immigrants in the 19th and early 20th centuries expanded the American Dream, including the opportunity to achieve financial success and social mobility through hard work and education.

- The colonial American Dream was built on property ownership and self-sufficiency.

- Immigration in the early 19th thru the early 20th centuries changed the American Dream to emphasize financial prosperity and social mobility through hard work and education.

- The post-Civil War American Dream included owning land as a sign of economic security and social standing.

- During the post-industrial and Gilded Ages, it transformed into amassing riches and material possessions by succeeding in school and the workplace.

- After World War I, the idea of sacrifice, hard work, and self-motivation became central to the American Dream, influenced by many Americans contributing and participating in the war.

- The brutal reality of World War I and the economic problems that followed the Great Depression led to disillusionment, social discontent, and a change in attitudes. Yet, the New Deal's implementation restored American confidence and economic stability. As a result, the American ideal eventually centered on upward mobility and the capacity for success.

- During World War II, it refocused on patriotism and battling for a brighter future. Racial discrimination was still a major issue at this time, making the American Dream extremely difficult for minorities. Notwithstanding these obstacles, the notion of the American Dream persisted as a strong incentive for many Americans and influenced the post-war prosperity of the nation.

- The American Dream then focused on attaining stability in the middle of the 20th century, when post-war optimism and the drive for conformity impacted society. It was centered on the nuclear family and the conventional ideal of owning a home, having a successful career, and giving your children a better life.

- The American Dream returned to building wealth in the post-Cold War era due to increased affluence and economic expansion.

- The current American Dream of the early 21st century is about adopting digital technologies and entrepreneurship in the Internet Era.

The American Dream can look different depending on whether you live in a city or a rural area. For folks in the city, the American Dream often means having access to education, career opportunities, and cultural experiences. Meanwhile, in rural areas, the American Dream is often tied to land ownership, agricultural success, and close-knit communities.

People's faith and spirituality can also impact the American Dream. It can take on different shapes for those raised in faith-based religious households and those raised in spiritual, non-religious households.

Understanding differing perspectives is crucial to comprehending current social environments and how people envision their versions of the American Dream.

Today's American Dream is no longer just about financial success but also about social responsibility and positive impact.

My life feels like a movie.

It's crazy to describe my life from where I was on that wintry New Year's Eve night, writing down where I was and who I thought I could be. I didn't know how to run a business. I would never even have considered writing a book.

When I look back at my time as a college baseball coach, I realize I was like a lot of Americans today, living in survival mode. I had a second job as a valet because I couldn't earn enough to live on an American newbie coach's salary, besides offering private lessons and working concessions. I was simply trying to get by day-to-day, trapped in what I thought was an

"I have had setbacks like any other entrepreneur, but I reached a point where my partners and I created RAD Diversified (RADD), which is thriving. RADD now has $200 million in AUMs, over 200 employees and contractors, and a Tribe of more than 5,000 investors."

unbreakable cycle, instead of beating, challenging, and unlocking the system to control my destiny.

I have had setbacks like any other entrepreneur, but I reached a point where my partners and I created RAD Diversified (RADD), which is thriving. RADD now has $200 million in AUMs,[12] over 200 employees and contractors, and a Tribe of more than 5,000 investors.

By telling you my journey, I hope you'll see where the foundation for this book comes from and how we at RADD are causing a seismic shift in how Americans think about money. We're not just playing the game. We're changing it.

Our mission is to help everyday Americans break free from the "Money Shackles" created by the "Freedom Traps" built into the system. With every step forward, we're empowering people to take control of their finances and create a better future for themselves and their families. It's a powerful feeling to know that we're making such a huge impact, and I can't wait to see how far we'll go in creating a financial movement.

Given my passion for that and my financial education, I believe that challenging the conventional way of living in America is an important step toward helping others succeed.

It's much more than keeping up with the Joneses, going to school, getting a job, working hard, and leaving a better life for one's children. This way of thinking creates a life that forces people into survival mode and puts them in constant financial insecurity, causing fear regarding investments and wealth.

Many have experienced the frustration of losing money to fraudulent schemes, economic downturns, or other investments. This fear

---

12   AUMs, or assets under management, refer to the total market value of all the assets and investments that a financial institution or individual manages on behalf of clients. Retrieved from https://www.investopedia.com/terms/a/aum.asp.

prevents people from making any financial decisions, leading to a loss of productivity and value.

This is not the kind of dream our country was founded on. It's natural to think we're in control of our destiny, but that's not the reality for many people today. Unfortunately, there are systems in place that can hold us back, even when we're doing everything right. It's a tough situation in which many people find themselves.

This is the "Freedom Trap" that creates "Money Shackles."

"Freedom Traps" are the cause resulting in the "Money Shackles."

"Freedom Traps" comes from a systematic process in America that won't allow people to break free from "Money Shackles" (self-imposed financial limitations). I'm talking about societal peer pressures, political propaganda, biased media, and the constant barrage of messages that only reinforce their ideas. Then there's a debt economy that people don't fully understand and institutional systems that don't teach real financial education.

Do everyday Americans know how to make their money work for them, harness their investments, and expand their earning potential?

It seems that few people are comprehensively talking about these topics. Such experts can advise on tax savings, investment strategies, and income growth. Lifestyle factors also play a critical role.

To achieve true financial freedom, individuals must understand and apply all these concepts simultaneously. Take these actions to unlock **The Four Freedom Principles**:

1. Save on Taxes

2.   Invest Wisely

3.   Increase Earning Potential

4.   Manage Lifestyle

However, it can be challenging to master all these components, and missing even one can impede progress toward true financial freedom.

Achieving financial freedom requires more than just a single skill or strategy. It requires a holistic understanding of personal finance and the daily discipline and commitment to implement these concepts. By doing so, anyone can move closer to a place of true freedom, independence, and security.

If you don't take action, you won't have control over your life.

My journey started by taking action on what I wrote down that frigid night as a valet, and when I decided to do things differently and listen to those who had already succeeded.

I had been coaching baseball for three years while valeting on the side but hit a rough financial path. Shortly after writing a story about my dream life, I left the valet gig for a regular job. I became a corporate recruiter/headhunter. I worked hard for the first six months after training, but I found myself in a cycle of working too hard for too few results and burning out. Wake up. Grind. Pass out.

My life lacked joy. I was unsatisfied.

Eventually, the head of training in that billion-dollar headhunting company where I worked gave me a wake-up call. He told me to stop doing things my way and start doing things his way. I started following his advice and found that I never had to work more than 30 to 40 hours a week again.

The company taught their employees to make endless phone calls daily, from 8 am to 5 pm. I did things differently. Instead of making many cold calls, I focused on building relationships with the right people. I worked from 2 pm to 7 pm every day, carefully building relationships, calling references, and reaching higher up the corporate chain. My approach was more organic and relationship-focused than the traditional, high-volume "pounding the pavement."

As a result, it turned out that I became the number-one headhunter in my field for two and a half years by simply listening and doing things differently. I was beginning to take control of my life.

After only six months of being a headhunter, I hit it big financially. I decided to quit coaching baseball, and with a $48,000 check sitting in my car's center console, I thought I had everything I needed to be happy.

The truth was, even with all that money, I still felt unfulfilled. I pulled over on the side of the highway, and tears came down my face when I realized that what I always thought the problem was in life wasn't the problem. It was the first time I asked God for answers, and it didn't happen.

> "The truth was, even with all that money, I still felt unfulfilled. I pulled over on the side of the highway, and tears came down my face when I realized that what I always thought the problem was in life wasn't the problem. It was the first time I asked God for answers, and it didn't happen."

No divine intervention or life-changing experience came to me.

You know, so much ego and what you carry within yourself when you reach these moments, you always think you have the answer, especially while stuck in survival mode. You think you know the problem that there's a dragon you can slay, but that wasn't the problem for me. It was my relationship with money that was the problem. The problem was not understanding it, not living with a purpose, or living my American Dream. I was shackled, even though I had money.

That day taught me that money is only part of the answer and that finding meaning in life is essential. If you're ready to pursue your American Dream, it's important to understand where you stand financially and take steps to build a life beyond financial gain.

I have a friend who sold his company for a lot of money, but shortly afterward, he was very close to ending it all because his journey had been based purely on money and financial gain. If you have nothing other than money in mind, you will never be satisfied. Money can be immediately gratifying, but it doesn't necessarily lead to a long-term, meaningful relationship with it.

You become a slave to money, confined by the "Money Shackles." When I became a headhunter for a billion-dollar company, I was finally making money, and it felt like the solution to everything. *I quickly realized that money was only part of the answer.*

Financial stability is crucial to overall well-being and can help improve mental health. Pursuing your American Dream involves balancing and building a strong financial foundation that supports finding purpose and meaning in your life.

These events in my past are one of the many aspects of why I want to build a dream beyond making money in the financial framework that makes up this guide and helps you take action and control your life.

I grew up poor and struggled financially. I know the lure money has and how having a lot of money can appear as the only solution to all your problems and the only key to achieving the American Dream, but it's not. While it is important, it's not the be-all-end-all. Focusing only on monetary gain can leave you feeling as empty and dissatisfied as a ghost.

The money conversation is a critical aspect of the American Dream. While some may assume that living paycheck-to-paycheck is an issue that only affects the working-class poor, the reality is that even high-income earners can be just one financial disaster away from that precarious existence.

"Doctors, business owners, professionals, lawyers, and multi-six-figure income household earners can all struggle with financial stability and security."

For many Americans, the American Dream is about upward mobility and achieving financial success through hard work and perseverance. However, for others, it's about providing their children with a better quality of life than they had. Whether to prioritize wealth accumulation or invest in their children's future is deeply personal and depends on an individual's values, goals, and financial circumstances. Ultimately, the money conversation reflects the competing priorities and challenges many face in pursuing a better life.

The decision to prioritize wealth accumulation or invest in one's children's future is just one of the many challenges people face in pursuing the American Dream. Financial challenges can be even more daunting for those living paycheck-to-paycheck or in survival mode. In this state, people constantly worry about the next ball to drop, the next problem to overcome, and the next issue they'll have to deal with while trying to figure out their next step. True independence and freedom simply don't exist in this mode of existence.

What could they do to achieve some type of independence?

We must return to the reality of what money can do for you. I hope to help you establish that financial framework to escape the "Freedom Trap" and break your "Money Shackles."

I admit that when I first started making money in the headhunting business, I struggled with what to do with it. By all expectations from my personal history, the worst is that I should have been an alcoholic or in jail. The best expectation would have been a college coach, but with kids and a broken marriage, and limited contact with my family.

Here's the good news: *I broke free from those constraints and continued to exceed the expectations most people had for me.*

Like many others, I expanded my knowledge and education, investing in workshops, seminars, and classes. I jumped at the opportunity when a "Thought Leader" asked me to coach and mentor his business professionals. Studying the business model of other "Thought Leaders" resulted in launching my consulting career.

I broke free.

Along with consulting, I enrolled in courses and started a side hustle in real estate. In addition, I consulted real estate companies on their marketing, advertising, staffing, and profit centers and quickly found success. Within six months, I went from consulting one company to ten companies, and within two years, I was consulting hundreds of entrepreneurs. In addition, I developed mentorship programs and guided over thousands of students toward success in business, entrepreneurship, and real estate.

I broke free.

As an entrepreneur, I have always relied on others to help me build and grow my business. A turning point came when we lost a client, and I had to lay off 22 hardworking employees without reason or cause of no fault of their own. We took that company from a few thousand dollars to eight figures, had met the CEO on a Monday, and on a Tuesday, he fired us. If the company who had hired us had researched the new CEO, they would have known this CEO had a track record of running successful companies this way. All we received was a half-hearted apology letter. I had already fired 22 people who had made a great team with the drive and mission to be successful.

Now, it's like being a ghost again, transparently floating through each person being fired. There's nothing, absolutely nothing, that can be said to make it better for them. Other than the standard, "I appreciate you, I'm sorry, I hope for the best." That's employer BS because those fired would rather just punch you in the face.

Even my business partner at the time didn't come to work for three days because he was so destroyed. That's when I knew things had to change.

Jonathan Cronstedt, a consultant I knew, was in the back of my mind during this event. Three years before, he had advised me, "Start your own business. You got all the tools, and though it may be hard, the rewards will make sense." He meant building my own company would pay off, even if it took more time to achieve this goal. After this event, I realized he was right. I could never allow someone else to control my business's future again or put my team in a similar situation.

I broke free.

The advice from the consultant proved to be a wake-up call for me. It made me realize that I needed to take action to build a more secure and sustainable future for myself and my employees and to break free from the "Money Shackles" that had been holding me back. I had to confront the reality that I was stuck in the "Freedom Trap" if I was going to achieve my version of the American Dream.

If I wanted to achieve the impact I knew I could make, I would have to take specific steps to break free from societal and industry standards and bridge the wealth gap to the super-rich. Only then could I live a life of true independence and freedom.

For many individuals who are not yet living the American Dream or do not realize they are caught in the system, the dream can feel broken. Despite this, I believe in the benefits of individual empowerment and ownership. It's time to stop listening to the mainstream media's bias telling you to live a life that isn't yours, and focus on building something special and unique. By adopting a wealth-building mindset and taking actionable steps to achieve financial freedom, you can create your unique version of the American Dream.

"Breaking free from financial limitations and carving out your niche requires effort and dedication, but it's worth it. True freedom, real individuality, and ownership over one's destiny are possible only by taking active steps toward breaking free from the 'Money Shackles.'"

According to a 2022 YouGov poll,[13] opinions about the American Dream vary widely. Only 43% of U.S. adult citizens believe the American Dream exists, while 35% do not, and 23% are uncertain. Interestingly, adults under 30 are the least likely to believe in the American Dream, with only 29% saying it exists, 40% saying it doesn't, and 31% unsure. Despite these differing opinions, it's clear that many people are seeking ways to create a better future for themselves and break free from financial limitations.

After a decade of consulting, I co-founded a coaching and mentoring company where I could help others achieve their financial goals. I started with a limited partnership under Regulation D in 2013, organizing live buying tours into auctions each month with a team of 5 people.

Establishing the business took two to three years of hard work, but I was determined to balance staying small, making more money, and growing it. Despite achieving financial comfort, I had a burning passion for business growth and helping the people I was educating.

Our main priority has always been taking care of our Tribe members or investors, building a strong reputation by putting all our efforts into

---

13   Sanders, L. 2022. *In 2022, do Americans believe in the 'American Dream'?* Retrieved from https://today.yougov.com/topics/politics/articles-reports/2022/07/14/do-americans-believe-american-dream.

each deal, and ensuring we did it right. Even today, our main focus remains to do every deal correctly.

Our focus on continuous growth and excellence was fueled even more when we launched the RADD Inner Circle and our Regulation A partnership in 2015. To gain confidence, my clients approached me with the idea of co-investing with them. They wanted to achieve success as a team.

Soon, I co-founded RAD Diversified REIT in 2019 to give accredited and non-accredited investors equal access. As RAD Diversified (RADD) continues to grow and evolve as a company, our mission is to be a leader in alternative investments.

Our focus is to provide financial freedom for thousands of Americans and create an active community of like-minded individuals.

This origin story is a testament to our commitment to investing in you and America.

It is time to take ownership and strive to live a fulfilling, purpose-driven existence because you were born with it.

I have seen countless individuals achieve some success but still find themselves unfulfilled and unsure of how to attain their true dreams. *Mere survival isn't an option, and neither is mediocrity.*

We provide hope, freedom, and community with a solid financial education. With this in mind, the question is, How can the American Dream be redefined to fit the realities of today's economy?

When your American Dream means building someone else's dream by either trying to keep up with the Joneses or letting mainstream media dictate how you're supposed to live, it's broken.

Choose what's most important to you and start building your dream.

> "Part of my American Dream is building collaborative financial freedom with others—not alone. All the wealth in the world doesn't mean anything if you're all alone."

To be clear, choosing to live your American Dream will do nothing without action. Failure to do so will leave you feeling unfulfilled.

Part of my American Dream is building collaborative financial freedom with others—not alone. All the wealth in the world doesn't mean anything if you're all alone.

If your idea is the stereotypical American Dream of a house with a white picket fence, two kids, two cars, and a family pet, that's great, but one size doesn't fit all. That's not the dream for many other Americans, right?

The word "diversified" in RADD represents all the different variations of what the American Dream could mean to you.

The American household has changed, and the dream should be attainable by everyone willing to work for it. As someone who has done it, nothing should deter you from achieving your version of the American Dream, whether as a single parent, a single person, or a grandparent raising kids.

The American Dream still has meaning but needs to adapt to our ever-changing economic landscape.

To Redefine the American Dream in today's economy, we must acknowledge that previous models may no longer work for everyone. *Financial freedom is the key.*

We must look beyond the traditional markers of success and focus on building a stronger financial foundation. It must enhance our values and enable us to pursue our passions and live the life we want.

In the following chapters, I will provide a comprehensive financial framework to help you achieve financial freedom, regardless of your situation.

Anybody who says life isn't better with money hasn't lived without money.

I'm sure you think I just said the opposite earlier, but remember, I said money is important, but not everything. It's obvious that people with money have problems just like people without it. However, how they face those problems is very different.

Money is not unattainable, mystical, or a magical part of the American Dream. Money is a controllable energy source, a currency of exchange for the goods and services we provide to the marketplace. It is impacted by our education and belief system.

With the right tools, investment vehicles, and mindset, we can expect better returns from our labor, experiences, ideas, and abilities. It is an active choice.

So where does the healthy money relationship start?

During a playful interaction with one of my kids' tutors, I instructed her to throw something away, and she jokingly responded by saying, · "Okay, rich guy." This comment caught me off guard, so I asked her what background she thought I came from growing up. She replied that I was born into generational wealth and a life of affluence. That couldn't have been further from the truth.

In reality, I didn't start with a silver spoon in my mouth. I have lived on my own since I was 16. My parents were addicts and passed away before they were 60 years old. I had to work hard to achieve financial stability.

This tutor's assumption about me was based on a stereotype that painted me as a person of privilege without any knowledge of my circumstances. This experience made me reflect on how our assumptions about people's financial situations can be far from the truth and the importance of avoiding financial stereotypes.

There's an underlying tension in America today.

Those who have the money often feel that those who do not have it are undeserving. Those without the money feel that those who have it are undeserving, too. These assumptions are flawed.

An individual's mindset, ability to handle finances, and the power of compounding over time (in either a good or bad direction), determine the direction of your American Dream.

I am Redefining the American Dream and challenging this perspective by showing how to finance your future and live a better, freer life.

I can attest to the "Money Shackles" that prevent people from achieving their financial goals, having personally experienced them and assisted many others in finding their financial freedom.

"A major contributor to peoples' 'Money Shackles' is a lack of financial education."

A major contributor to peoples' 'Money Shackles' is a lack of financial education.

People fail to accumulate riches because of their—

- inability to handle or leverage money
- fear of taking chances
- fear of failure
- fear of losing money, such as investing in the stock marketor beginning a business
- The inability to stay focused on what really matters.

The lack of discipline and commitment can also prevent people from achieving financial freedom. Establishing good money habits and building a solid financial foundation takes time and consistency. You must be willing to do the work and be patient to achieve the returns.

The 'Freedom Trap' in America is a system designed to eliminate or severely limit your ability to build wealth.

Some examples include:

"The 'Freedom Trap' in America is a system designed to eliminate or severely limit your ability to build wealth."

- The cost of a college degree vs. earning capacity over time.

- Trusting your hard-earned money to a financial advisor who hasn't achieved financial success themselves.

- Investing in the Stock Market Roller Coaster, including using corporate benefits and retirement plans that don't align with your values and goals.

- Hyper-Consumerism influences to encourage you to spend money you don't have on things you don't need.

- Inflation outpacing your income earning potential.

- Understanding that taxes are one of the major impediments to wealth creation.

- Starting a business with limited capital and/or business knowledge.

Many of these approaches have broken the American Dream and may not be the best path to getting where you want to go, but there's another option:

"Becoming a Fractional Owner in alternative investments and diversifying your portfolio."
—Dutch Mendenhall

I discovered a different approach to debt that transforms it into a powerful tool for financial success.

People can quickly achieve breakthroughs by collaborating, investing, or creating businesses. I came to realize there are alternatives to investing with a financial advisor or in the stock market. Traditional investment methods are not the only path to success. The key to unlocking opportunities is to build relationships and recognize which ones are worth pursuing. Identifying and working with the right people is essential for achieving your goals.

Here's the truth — Building wealth is more than earning money. It's about having a stable financial foundation that provides you with the freedom to live the life you desire.

Understanding the framework for achieving financial freedom is the solution to freeing yourself from all other types of "Money Shackles." You must acquire the knowledge and skills to continue increasing wealth and achieving the American Dream.

Start by learning how to make your path with these **Building Blocks**.

Self-education: Assess where you currently are regarding your income and expenses. Then begin acquiring the financial knowledge and skills needed to achieve your American Dream. With the right knowledge and skills, you'll be able to determine which options will enable you to build a solid financial foundation. One of the best investments you'll make is to invest regularly in self-education. As you grow, so should your income. Knowledge is only potential power until it's put into action!

Invest Savings: Having a reliable and consistent source of income from your investments leads to financial security. The key is to put your savings to work in investments that compound and cycle your money in diverse assets. Wise financial decisions lead to the security and abundance you desire.

Options: Having greater comfort in life comes from having access to abundant money through savings and purchasing power. This gives us options to have more for ourselves, our families, and impact (charity). The pathway to building this wealth is to get your money working for you. Study the different investment vehicles to provide you with many options.

Lifestyle from Investments: To understand financial freedom, you need to consider first what lifestyle you want to achieve, then be able to earn that amount of money (preferably more). I suggest that most of the money you need for that lifestyle comes from your investments (passive and passive residual income).

You can create your ideal future, just like I did.

To do so, you should organize your plans according to the **Freedom Chart**

In the Freedom Chart, there are four main block components to achieving financial freedom to Redefine your American Dream in the Freedom Chart. Your living **costs, income**, **investments**, and the scale of your **freedom** mobility.

Pretty self-explanatory, right?

Freedom Chart

```
              |
    COST      |   INCOME
 _____|_____
              |
  INVESTMENTS |   FREEDOM
              |
```

The gaps between these blocks to financial freedom are your lifestyle gaps.

You probably wouldn't have much maneuverability at $30,000 a year compared to someone with $100,000 a year. Still, it is doable for anyone of any class bracket wanting to expand their earning potential.

When you start taking control of your financial situation, making smart alternative decisions and making money and debt work for you, you're investing in your future to earn more.

This is how the lifestyle gaps in the Freedom Chart will help you understand where to reorganize and balance your options. Each lifestyle gap serves a different purpose:

- The basic *lifestyle choices gap*, which is ever-changing, based on your living **costs** and **income**.

- The *permanent lifestyle gap* you could achieve when you include your **investments** in your living **costs**, which will help compound your financial freedom over time.

- The *investment-based lifestyle gap* is determined by how much **income** you receive to scale your **freedom**, which will help you grow into a good investor (Chapter 7).

- *Shackles broken* when your capital from **income** and **investments** exceeds your living **costs**, which helps you to become a great investor (Chapter 11).

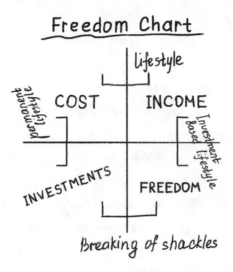

You'll want to use the Freedom Chart to break your Money Shackles. To ensure that, you need to do only three things:;

- Keep your living **costs** *down*, ideally below your total capital.
- Your total capital is the *total value* of your **income** and **investment** returns.
- The moment you can *sustainably live* on your investments or a small percentage of your total capital, you have begun breaking your shackles to **freedom**.

I used to feel that building wealth was an unknown.

My focus was on something other than becoming an entrepreneur, creating a movement, or making a sweeping impact that could alter how the nation approaches investments and the American Dream.

Challenges that prevent people from investing include a lack of knowledge or money, risk aversion, fear, and time constraints.

If you have the right resources and guidance, investing can be accessible to anyone. By educating myself and seeking assistance, I now have the confidence to invest my money and work towards achieving my financial goals.

Now, by many people's standards, looking at my current situation, I've achieved considerable amounts of success. On that cold New Year's night, I never could have imagined where I would be today. My focus was on something other than becoming an entrepreneur, creating a movement, or making a sweeping impact that could alter how the nation approaches investment and finances.

Yet, that's what I've done.

By reflecting on my life and purpose, I broke free from societal expectations and became the person I knew I was meant to be. My story is important because it provides a roadmap for others who may feel lost or disconnected from the American Dream we've all been sold for generations.

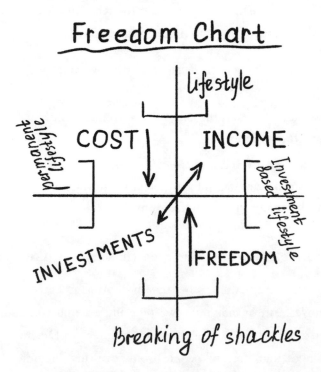

Here's the thing—your future belongs to YOU. It's about something other than keeping up with anyone else or meeting society's expectations. You have the power to create the life you truly want to live.

I've gone from being humbled and surprised at having achieved everything I wrote on that cold New Year's night to an expectation of destiny and future that allows me to live my Redefined American Dream.

My dream is to make an impact in every aspect of my life. I am a husband and father that is always present and a faithful follower of my path.

I'm fulfilling our destiny daily with our movement where Americans can truly start believing in themselves, their country, and owning the freedoms we've been given. I'm living my Redefined American Dream. You can live yours too.

Chapter Review

If you'd like to practice what you've learned in this chapter, I invite you to check out the exercises at this link:
https://therad.com/moneyshackles/workbook

The chapter exercises encourage you to define where you are currently and your vision of the American Dream, take actionable steps by creating a personal financial framework, and evaluate your financial freedom according to the Four Freedom Principles and Freedom Chart.

1. Challenge the conventional way of living in America and take control of your financial situation to break free from the "Money Shackles" and "Freedom Traps" that can hold you back from living your Redefined American Dream.

2. The American Dream has evolved, starting with breaking free from colonial governance, growing to encompass financial success and social mobility, and now social responsibility and positive impact. It can look different depending on where you live, your faith, and your upbringing, but understanding differing perspectives is crucial to comprehending current social environments.

3. To achieve true financial freedom and break free, you need to:

    •   Apply the ***Four Freedom Principles*** to strategically save on taxes, invest wisely, increase earning potential, and manage lifestyle.

    •   Your ***Building Blocks to Financial Freedom*** should

include a strong foundation through daily discipline and a holistic understanding of personal finance. Then make informed, smart alternative investment decisions and put money and debt to work for you through the power of compounding and cycling investment capital through other investments.

- Apply the *Freedom Chart* to balance your lifestyle choices, income, living costs, investments, and financial freedom.

4. You deserve to live a fulfilling, purpose-driven life by Redefining the American Dream to fit your values and passions and to achieve financial freedom through a comprehensive financial framework. Money is important, but not everything, and with the right tools and mindset, it is an active choice to attain better returns from your labor, experiences, ideas, and abilities.

5. To achieve financial freedom, you need to challenge assumptions about people's financial situations, avoid financial stereotypes, and work to build a healthy money relationship, which is often limited by the "Money Shackles" and the "Freedom Trap" created by a lack of financial education, fear of taking chances, hyper-consumerism, inflation, taxes, and investing in the wrong places.

Have you been sold someone else's American Dream? You may have been sold someone else's American Dream if your goals and aspirations have been influenced by societal pressures or expectations rather than your desires and passions, which can impede you from achieving true financial freedom.

CHAPTER 2

YOUR REDEFINED AMERICAN DREAM STARTS COMING TRUE TODAY

How does financial security contribute to a fulfilling life aligned with your values and goals?

To live the American Dream, you must understand the battle to achieve it.

It's not only about having a dream—it's the journey to get there. That journey is a battle you have to be willing to fight for to attain. The road ahead may not be easy and will require some serious changes, beginning with acknowledging the value of financial education.

Consider how you manage money, invest, and make decisions to keep your money working for you to sustain the lifestyle you desire and the legacy or community impact you wish to leave behind.

The middle class has been shrinking for decades. Fewer and fewer Americans can live the American Dream. COVID-19 only worsened it.

- According to a Pew Research Center report, adults in middle-income households have decreased from 61% to 51% in under 50 years.[14]

- The Bureau of Labor Statistics has noted an increase in the working poor between 2019-2020, as it went up from 7.6 million to 9.6 million.[15] Yet, according to the Bureau, there's expected to be a 1-2% drop in under 10 years, and that's not seeing the overall economic growth.

- A Pew report found that those in upper-income households increased from 14% to 20%, and adults in lower-income households increased from 25% to 29% between 1971-2019.

Here's the picture: fewer people in the middle class and more people in the working poor, but there is more money and more opportunity to access that upper income than ever before.

There's progress being made, and you can break through and achieve financial independence with the right approach. That means stepping out of your comfort zone, taking risks, and pursuing your passions with all your energy.

Don't miss your chance to seize opportunities and reach your financial goals. You can thrive in the hard times. Many Americans don't understand their financial options or how to use them. They're unaware of the paths to take. There's a shortage of education.

You will learn how to build wealth. Don't settle for the status quo. You have what it takes to escape the "Freedom Trap." I will guide you

---

14   Kochhar, R and Sechopoulos, S. 2022. *How the American middle class has changed in the past five decades.* Retrieved from https://www.pewresearch.org/fact-tank/2022/04/20/how-the-american-middle-class-has-changed-in-the-past-five-decades/.

15   Monthly Labor Review. 2022. *Projections overview and highlights, 2021-2031.* Retrieved from https://www.bls.gov/opub/mlr/2022/article/projections-overview-and-highlights-2021-31.htm.

through this. Together, we will explore the American Dream and how it has evolved. We'll identify your interpretation of the American Dream and discuss the importance of pursuing your passions to create a *purpose-driven existence.*

You may not believe me when I say you can thrive during hard times despite feeling overwhelmed or uncertain about changing your current lifestyle.

Are you feeling uncertain about it? It's understandable if you resist certain advice and prefer to stick to your current lifestyle. After all, it feels safe and predictable, and going against the norm may appear daunting. Yet, consider this: by embracing change and working to make adjustments, you open yourself up to new possibilities and opportunities for growth.

If you're living paycheck-to-paycheck and looking to improve your financial situation, assessing and conquering these vulnerabilities is important.

Since reading the last chapter, have you considered your interpretation of the American Dream and asked yourself some foundational life-building questions, such as:

- Where in life are you now?
- Did you realize you are chasing someone else's dream, unsure where to start, and not fully seeing what you want to improve your life and purpose come to fruition?

Once you've answered these questions, it's time to explore your passions and interests. Seek guidance from successful people in your life and ask about their journey and the role their values and passions have played in navigating their American Dream.

My understanding of this evolution came from my humble beginnings as a poor kid. When I later became a college baseball coach I worked excessively long hours. I then realized that this level of indentured servitude was not worth its financial challenges. Then when I started making money as a headhunter, I soon realized it wasn't just about money. It was something else. It took starting consulting and creating businesses, making other people successful, to truly see it was about control or ownership of my dreams. The thing is, the American Dream has evolved and is the way we can build wealth.

Here's one of the RADD keys to breaking through this evolution to start your journey: *Adopting the collaborative investment or co-investing attitude to achieving financial freedom.*

I believe the most effective approach to achieving my investment goals has been to invest alongside individuals who share similar objectives and beliefs. I may exchange tactics and insights that move me closer to reaching my goals by forming a network of partners and investors. Together, we can reduce risks and create a plan with a high possibility of long-term success. Working together is key, and by adopting this perspective, I'm convinced that I can enhance my life and the lives of people around me.

As you reflect on your journey, you will realize that you have frequently had to Redefine your dream. Growing up, you probably were taught that success meant having a good job, a nice house, and a family. As you grew older, you started questioning whether these societal pressures and norms were what you wanted out of life.

It wasn't until you reached adulthood that you realized that financial problems and challenges were not what you truly desired. You wanted more. You wanted to make a difference in the lives of others and achieve your true desires. This meant looking into investing.

It took learning the hard way that success was not just about money or being the head honcho. It's about going through the battles and the journey to find what truly matters to you. I closed down a seven-figure business because it was causing drama and would never give me mental freedom. My partners didn't have the right integrity or alignment for me.

When it comes to investing, it has always been a massive challenge for me to find the right Tribe to partner with. Finding the right people with the same values and goals is crucial. This has been a challenging journey for me. I have cut ties with close friends and business partners to rebuild and reinvent myself.

These experiences have strengthened me, and I have learned to be more cautious in selecting the people I work with to achieve my goals. Trust is essential in any business relationship. Building it takes time and effort, but it's ultimately worth it.

Reinventing yourself requires rebuilding to achieve your version of the American Dream. You may have to cut close friends and business partners from the equation to build what you want.

It isn't just about finding the right people, developing the right mindset, and investing in yourself. Believe in yourself and your abilities, even when others don't. Take risks and make sacrifices, It is worth it.

What has to happen for you to transition from surviving with your "Money Shackles" to thriving in your newly Redefined American Dream?

My friends Sarita Lee and Kevin Mantell have each undergone their own challenges, but they managed to transform themselves and Redefine their aspirations. Reflecting on their journeys, I see how reinvention is crucial to the American Dream. They both had a clear mission, and we're committed to achieving their goals. Kevin pursued a career in real estate, while Sarita aimed to leave a legacy by building a circle of dependable people around her. Their values and priorities are essential for anyone who wants to achieve their dreams. To make progress, you need to understand your purpose, focus on it, and determine the path you want to follow.

Sarita is an analyst for the state of California and also a Navy reservist currently on duty in Hawaii. A single mom who has been through a divorce, she wanted to build her American Dream by trying to find someone she could trust and build a legacy for her children. Her experiences have made her cautious about trusting others, especially in the real estate industry. Despite her reservations, Sarita has a good relationship with her ex-husband, Ethan, whom she trusts. She was able to find an individual who could assist her with her real estate needs, thanks to his help.

"Just after my divorce, I felt I was starting from ground zero," Sarita says. She remembers asking herself, "What can I do to ensure that my daughter and my grandchildren are taken care of?" She didn't want them to start from scratch. Her goal is to grow her net worth so that she can leave investment properties to her and her grandchildren. "I'm not trying to be a real estate mogul," Sarita says. "I want to have enough long-term wealth so that when I'm gone, my family is cared for, and they don't have to start from poverty."

Kevin has a rich professional background, having spent 20 years managing luxury jewelry and watch stores in some of the most upscale malls in New York City. In 2015, he took a job that required him to travel across the country selling high-end watches and another job selling diamonds. Although this meant spending most of his week on the road, he prioritized being a committed father, working hard to create a legacy for himself and his family.

"Reinvention is a challenging process," Kevin says, "but it's all part of the American Dream. I decided to take the leap and embark on a new journey, even though it meant moving away from my children (temporarily) and entering a completely different industry," he says.

"When I started my journey, I traveled to 25 different states and was on a plane almost every day. Being away from my children was tough, but I made sure to stay connected with them as much as possible. My own experiences as a young child losing my parents made me even more determined to be there for my kids," says Kevin.

> "The focal point is how you can get there. Choose. No matter what happens, make a choice."

When COVID-19 hit in 2020, Kevin was living in Massachusetts, renting a house near his children. With the spread of the pandemic, everything changed instantly.

"I was blindsided when COVID hit," Kevin says. "All of the stores I worked with suddenly shut down. I received two phone calls in one day—one for diamonds and one for watches—informing me that my business was being shut down due to the supply chain interruption and stores being closed, with most Tribe members staying at home."

The sudden change in circumstances left Kevin with a lot of uncertainty. He recalls, "I was really worried about how I was going to generate income and provide for my children. I started looking for jobs in Massachusetts and New Jersey, where I'm originally from."

Kevin eventually found a job in the home improvement business in New Jersey. "I had a lot of options to choose from," he says, "but at the time, the world was shut down, and the only jobs available were in essential businesses."

Sarita and Kevin have faced their challenges head-on and are working towards building a better future for themselves and their families.

Sometimes, we may need to divert from our original path, but staying focused on our focal point is crucial to reach our goals. Reinvention is a part of the journey toward achieving the American Dream, and it can happen at any point in our lives. As I continue my journey, I'm inspired by my friends' stories, and I stay focused on my purpose to achieve my goals.

Reinvention is part of the American Dream.

You wake up early, ready to tackle the day ahead. You've been thinking a lot about your future lately, and you know it's time to start taking action. You want to leave a legacy and impact the world but are unsure how. Do you know it starts with securing your financial future but with many different investment options and instruments available?

You start by doing your research. You read up on alternative investment options, from peer-to-peer lending, real estate, cryptocurrency, etc. You talk to financial advisors and analyze to determine which investments are right for you. You know there is no one-size-fits-all solution, but with careful planning and analysis, you can find the right mix of investments to help you achieve your goals.

Yet, it's not just about money. Finding purpose and meaning in life is just as important as financial security. You spend time reflecting on your personal goals and passions, trying to figure out how you can make a real impact on the world. It could be through volunteer work, starting your own business, or pursuing a career that allows you to help others.

The American Dream is not unattainable. Taking advantage of programs and policies that support financial literacy, education, affordable housing, healthcare, and education can open up pathways to success for everyone. With the right investments and mindset, anyone can start from wherever they are to build their version of the American Dream.

The inspiring stories of Kevin's and Sarita's reinvention highlight the importance of hard work, perseverance, and financial planning in achieving success. However, it's important to acknowledge that not everyone has had the same opportunities, and their stories shed light on the challenges facing America's shrinking middle class and working poor. Despite these obstacles, Kevin's and Sarita's stories serve as a reminder that it's possible to overcome adversity and achieve one's dreams with determination and a strong sense of purpose.

The focal point is how you can get there. Choose. No matter what happens, make a choice.

The Financial Decision Tree is essential, and I explore this further below. You know, you're trying to be successful, and you make a decision. If it's the wrong decision, you might go in the wrong direction, but then you realize it's wrong, and you can re-steer toward the right one. By making decisions, you'll eventually get to the right decision. Yet, if you never decide, you never leave the starting point. It's time to start the Financial Decision Tree.

It is better to make a good decision than stick with a bad one. We should strive to become skilled in making decisions. Our decision-making toolkit provides the tools and thought processes necessary for this objective. It guides us in choosing our path and arriving at decisions with confidence.

The "path" is important.

When you're headed in the right direction, things start to flow. There will still be challenges, but opportunities will appear, and hidden connections will emerge that you never knew existed. This is because destiny is guiding you down the path of least resistance. When not on the correct path, everything will wither away. Choose a path, and start down it to discover the right one.

You might recognize it's wrong, but that Financial Decision Tree will get you further.

You can wait for life to happen and allow others or the universe to tell you where to go, but the thing is, you're not choosing your path. You're living a life of reaction versus action. That's part of the status quo, the "Money Shackles" of your "Freedom Trap" buried in the conjecture of life. Buried in the circumstance of your life.

Did you have a kid when you were too young for parenthood? Did you drop out of school? Do you have a criminal record? What is your excuse? Will you choose to be victimized by your past, or will you use it as a stepping stone toward success?

To a large extent, American society has a victim mentality that prevents individuals from being proactive and taking control of their lives. Instead of actively choosing a path of reinvention and achieving their Redefined American Dream, many people allow themselves to be victims of life. This mindset undermines the resilience and self-reliance essential to achieving success and prosperity.

My story of the American Dream is what I build. I create, conquer, accomplish, and define my destiny. No one defines my destiny. I failed

to become a college baseball player, but it taught me never to allow anyone else to control my destiny. I choose to be a part of what created my
strength and power.

The "Freedom Income" starting point is to generate cash flow exceeding expenses

Here's one simple step to reinvent yourself: build your assets before you buy your lifestyle or build your legacy.

Let's get into money and how money works that can help you leave the legacy you are making an impact within your Redefined American Dream.

Financial freedom is the goal that many people strive for, but it requires making smart decisions when it comes to managing money. Making good financial decisions can be challenging, but there is a tool that can help – the **Financial Decision Tree**.

A Financial Decision Tree is a tool that helps to evaluate options based on a set of criteria. It will provide a clear and objective way to effectively make smart choices and reach financial goals in the context of the money conversation toward financial freedom. This structured approach to decision-making can help with your **emotional intelligence** to avoid emotional or impulsive decisions, especially if you may feel overwhelmed or unsure about how to get started. Use the Financial Decision Tree as a starting point to attain your "Freedom Income" by creating and enacting plans to generate monthly cash flow that exceeds your monthly lifestyle expenses.

To begin, it involves outlining your **investment goals and values**. This is your focal point and path of reinvention, and will help you define your **investment process** later.

Next is to understand where you stand in achieving a **Freedom Income**, where your cash flow exceeds your expenses. The starting point is knowing your:

- Monthly Income
- Monthly Expenses
- Monthly Savings
- Monthly Debt Services

- Monthly Investments' Net Value

Let's dive deeper into your starting point.

Begin creating a table that outlines a set of criteria that you will use to evaluate options. For example, allocating a paycheck might include expenses, savings, debt payments, and investments. The next step is to list each option that will help increase cash flow being considered under each category and assign a score for each criterion. The scores can be based on a scale of 0 to 10, with 10 being the best possible score. After you have evaluated all available options, combine the scores to identify the optimum choice for your goals.

Money Buckets, similar to envelope budgeting, is a powerful financial tool that goes beyond just keeping track of income, expenses, and savings. You can easily prioritize and manage your financial goals by allocating funds into different categories. However, it's important to note the money buckets I'm suggesting are not used to become debt-free. Instead, use them to plan and save for investments that generate long-term wealth. Whether it's planning for someone's educational future, a down payment on a property, or a portfolio of diversified assets, a well-planned and executed money bucket strategy can help you build wealth over time. So don't be afraid to try it and see how it can benefit your financial future.

Another part of your decision-making process is to address the topic of debt. Managing your debt and making it work for you is crucial to succeed financially. Today's people are taught that to achieve the American Dream, they must go into debt, buy a house and car, and invest in the stock market while trying to pay off their loans. This approach is counterproductive as it only leads to financial distress rather than achieving the dream.

The American "Money Shackles" are real. The traditional American values of land ownership, property investment, community involvement, productivity, and the pursuit of purpose remain relevant today.

To be successful financially, it's important to use debt as a tool for success instead of failure. So make a debt bucket. Use debt to make money, invest in assets that grow, expand income, and specialize in education or own rental property.

Dividing your money into buckets for different purposes is a valuable skill set. With investments also as one of your criteria for increasing cash flow, putting them into smaller buckets of high to low-risk options may be helpful as a **risk management** strategy. It's important to understand that not all investments carry the same level of risk.

That's why we also need to think about dividing our investment portfolio into different **Risk Buckets**, such as:

- high-risk/high-reward come with significant potential for growth, but can be volatile.

- high-risk/low-reward offer minimal returns with hazardous effects, and are never the bucket you will want to plan for.

- low-risk/high-reward investments also offer good returns and are less perilous.

- low-risk/low-reward investments provide little potential for growth but are safer.

- moderate-risk investments fall somewhere in between.

You can use the Financial Decision Tree to decide your important buckets and financial strategies and evaluate options based on your unique financial situation and goals. Expanding your earning abilities with the Financial Decision Tree will create a new exchange of money in your life, to ensure your **financial performance** delivers. It will provide you with the skills needed to do more. If you never earn enough, it may put you constantly back into the "Money Shackles."

Kevin Mantell did everything right from a traditional financial planning and investment perspective, but even he was not immune to the impact of the pandemic. When the stores he worked with shut down, his income stream disappeared overnight, leaving him anxious and unsettled. He was one financial disaster away from living paycheck to paycheck. Kevin pivoted to a new industry and made strategic investments that allowed him to survive and thrive.

"I'm working now six days a week, sometimes seven, twelve to fourteen hours a day," he says. Eventually, he makes enough money to allow him more time with his family. "I make about five times the amount of money I used to make in the jewelry business, which allows me to fund my real estate deals. My plan was to align myself with real estate and home improvement to build a portfolio, to take the money I generate from a W-2 job, put it into my investments with RADD, and then eventually have passive income coming in through that."

Kevin adds, "That's where I am now. I'm doing quite well financially, and I take those earnings and I put them into my investments with RADD. I have money with a financial planner and some with my self-directed IRA 401(k). When I separated the two, I pretty much started out with equal amounts. The money that has been generated with RADD in my self-directed account is about six times larger than the money that has been generated by my financial planner, with all his initials and degrees and fees, and so forth."

Build your assets as Kevin did. He invested in two places: his 401(k) and RADD. He picked a traditional investment and a diversified alternative investment. Kevin recognized the importance of investing in his financial literacy, which led him to discover RADD.

While Sarita is not a highly successful investor, she has succeeded with RAD Diversified. She often says she "pays pros to be pros." It is important to note that being a successful investor takes time and effort, and the word "highly" should not be used loosely to describe someone's investment success.

With the right mindset and investments, anyone can begin to change their life for the better and build their version of the American Dream -- regardless of where they are starting from.

As you work toward your goals, remember the importance of negotiating with creditors and avoiding further debt. Financial freedom is key to a lasting legacy, which means smartly managing your debts and investments. Collaborate with others, diversify your investments, and seek new opportunities to help you achieve your goals.

Ultimately, you know that making an impact and leaving a legacy is more than just acquiring wealth. It's about finding meaning and purpose and using your resources to help others. By investing wisely, negotiating with creditors, and pursuing your passions, you can achieve both financial freedom and personal fulfillment. And in doing so, you can leave a lasting legacy that will inspire others for generations.

Chapter Review

If you'd like to practice what you've learned in this chapter, I invite you to check out the exercises at this link: https://therad.com/moneyshackles/workbook

The chapter exercises encourage you to define your focal point by making choices that lead to your reinvention, use the Financial Decision Tree to establish your starting point and prioritize your money and risk buckets, and identify and list the risks and changes that will have you step out of your comfort zone and manage your money differently to break through and achieve financial independence

1. To achieve the American Dream, you must be willing to fight the battle to attain it, which includes acknowledging the value of financial education and changing how you manage your money, invest, and make decisions. Progress is still being made, and opportunities to break through and achieve financial independence by stepping out of your comfort zone, taking risks, and pursuing your passions. To do so, you may need to redefine your dream, seek guidance from successful people, and adopt a collaborative investment attitude to achieve long-term success.

2. To achieve your dreams, you need to secure your financial future by researching and analyzing different investment options to find the right mix of investments and mindset to achieve your goals. It's important to also find purpose and meaning in life. Remember, deciding and taking action is better than staying at the starting point. The process includes:

- Finding the focal point is how you can get to your dreams. Your focal point is about making choices.

- These choices will lead to your reinvention.

- To be more confident in your reinvention, use the *Financial Decision Tree*. A tool to evaluate options on a set of criteria.

- After you have evaluated your priorities, categorize your budget and goals by allocating funds into *Money Buckets*.

- Then, within your investment bucket, categorize your portfolios into *Risk Buckets* to ensure your strategies deliver the financial performance you seek.

3. Achieving success and fulfilling your Redefined American Dream includes actively choosing your path and taking control of your life to avoid being a victim of circumstance. You build and achieve success on your own terms by creating, conquering, accomplishing, and defining your destiny. Investing in yourself is also an important investment that will pay off for the rest of your life.

How does financial security contribute to a fulfilling life aligned with your values and goals? To achieve financial freedom and a fulfilling life aligned with your values and goals, you must understand the journey toward the American Dream and be willing to fight for it. This involves adopting a collaborative investment attitude, redefining your dream, choosing the right path in life, managing money wisely, and investing in yourself to expand your earning abilities.

CHAPTER 3

ASSESSING YOUR
MONEY PERSONALITY

How does your relationship with money affect your financial decision-making?

I come from a background of poverty and financial instability, but I had a mission to rise above my circumstances and discover a new way of thinking about money. My journey of self-discovery led me to recognize the importance of understanding my money personality and using that knowledge to make informed financial decisions.

Many of you can relate to financial instability and uncertainty struggles—being in constant survival mode. It's a common dilemma that can cause stress and anxiety, but it's important to remember that we have the power to change our financial situation. By understanding your money personality, you can take control of your financial decisions and move towards a more stable future.

The journey takes time and effort, but the rewards are invaluable!

I'm a natural "Risk-Taker and Flyer"—two aspects of my money personality—and I've

> "The journey takes time and effort, but the rewards are invaluable!"

channeled my energy into smart investments that have allowed me to grow my wealth and create a better future for myself and my family. While I understand the allure of making big money, I also know the importance of smart spending and investment strategies.

My experience has inspired me to help others financially by offering personalized investment strategies that align with their money personalities. Self-discovery is a fundamental part of the American Dream, and it starts with understanding your true self, including your money personality. Identifying and working with your money personality can make all the difference in achieving financial stability and success. Let me help you achieve financial success by finding your money personality type and creating a plan that aligns with your goals and values. With my knowledge and your eagerness to learn, we'll take your financial journey to new heights.

My upbringing didn't foster a healthy relationship with money. I grew up with parents who rode a financial rollercoaster filled with loops, highs, and lows. They transitioned from being functioning addicts to becoming dysfunctioning addicts. This forced me to live on my own at the age of 16. At 18, I had my first car repossessed.

At 22, I spent a night in jail for not paying a speeding ticket. I lost another car to unpaid parking tickets. I didn't understand what credit was or fully understand finances. So if you think your financial future is locked, I'm a testament that change is possible and necessary, and you can Redefine your American Dream.

To achieve long-term financial success and leave a lasting impact, you need to understand your money habits and tendencies deeply.

I will explore money personalities further later in this chapter. Know that by taking inventory of your assets and gaining insight into your money personality, you can identify your strengths and weaknesses and work towards making positive changes. Admitting faults and striving for improvement is essential in this process.

A deep self-analysis can lead to a better financial future and a fulfilling life, which enables you to benefit yourself and pass your legacy on to others. To further your journey toward financial success, it may be helpful to understand the **Five Money Personality** types—which are generally known: Spenders, Flyers, Security Seekers, Savers, and Risk Takers.

Everyone has a unique money personality that influences their financial decisions and behaviors. Understanding and cultivating a healthy relationship with money is important, just one of many energy sources contributing to a fulfilling life. Various factors, such as upbringing and experiences, shape your money personality, which remains consistent throughout your life.

Identifying your money personality is crucial to achieving financial stability and success. Understanding your money personality means you can make informed financial decisions that align with your values and goals. Similarly to how people have a constant love language, it's important to identify your money personality so that you can make choices that help you succeed financially.

Identifying your money personality requires an honest self-assessment of your financial tendencies. Are you a Spender or a Saver? Do you prefer investing, gambling, keeping your money in a savings account, hiding under the bed, or getting a thrill from making purchases? Knowing your tendencies will help you create a financial plan that aligns with your goals.

Let's examine the different money personalities and how they shape our financial decisions.

- **Spender**, someone who enjoys instant gratification and may struggle with saving money or sticking to a budget.

- **Flyer**, someone who isn't motivated by money and avoids conflict regarding money.

- **Security-Seeker**, someone who seeks to make their money work for them by analyzing investment opportunities but needs safety to take calculated risks to grow their wealth.

- **Saver**, someone who prioritizes saving money over spending it. Savers are always looking for ways to reduce expenses and may struggle to let go of their hard-earned money.

- **Risk-Taker**, someone who enjoys taking risks and may be willing to invest in high-risk opportunities for the potential of high rewards.

To determine your money personality, begin by getting real with yourself and looking hard at your spending habits. Start by keeping track of where your money is going and identifying areas where you could cut back. Another way to figure out your financial tendencies is to take a money personality test—it might give you some insights you hadn't considered before.

As a successful investor, I know the importance of having a financial plan tailored to one's personality type. Spendthrifts must focus on creating a budget emphasizing savings, while Savers must find opportunities to invest their money for maximum returns. Identifying your money personality type will determine your financial decisions, whether you are a Risk-Taker or a Security-Seeker.

Money is commonly cited as the greatest argument, point of conflict, and reason for divorce. The five money personalities are a helpful tool for understanding one's financial tendencies. They are similar to the five love languages that Gary Chapman writes about in his book "The Five Love Languages." While the five money personalities and the five love languages are two different concepts, they can complement each other in a relationship.

Financial disagreements in relationships can range from differing attitudes towards spending and saving to disagreements over financial priorities to conflicts over debt and financial goals. Research has shown that couples with different approaches to money who don't communicate about their finances are more likely to experience conflict and divorce. Some studies suggest financial disagreements are a stronger predictor of divorce than other common relationship issues, such as disagreements over chores or in-laws.

According to recent surveys, money fights are the second leading cause of divorce, behind infidelity.

- A survey by SunTrust Bank found that financial stress was the leading cause of stress in relationships, with 35% of respondents citing money as the primary cause of stress.[16]

- Another National Endowment for Financial Education survey found that 59% of respondents reported financial problems as a primary factor in their marriage or relationship breakdown.[17]

- Couples who reported disagreeing about money once a week were over 30% more likely to get divorced than couples who reported disagreeing about money a few times a month.

Couples can improve their relationships by discussing their financial habits and goals and creating a plan that works for both partners.

This involves setting a budget, agreeing on financial priorities, and being open and honest about money issues. Seeking outside help, such as a financial planner or counselor, can be beneficial. Additionally, understanding each other's money personality can help couples make decisions together and find common ground. However, having two different money personalities can pose a challenge, such as when one partner is a Saver prioritizing security, and the other is a Risk-Taker. Maintaining a harmonious relationship despite differences in financial tendencies is important.

---

16   Suknanan, J. 2023. *54% of people believe a partner with debt is a reason to consider divorce - here are other ways debt may affect your marriage.* Retrieved from https://www.cnbc.com/select/national-debt-relief-survey-debt-reason-for-divorce/.

17   n/d. 2021. *The Harris Poll: Financial Infidelity Survey.* Retrieved from https://www.nefe.org/Press-Room/NEFE-Survey-Reveals-the-Hidden-Costs-of-Financial-Infidelity.aspx.

One of the great accelerators of wealth is being on the same page with your spouse. It's important to have conversations about how we want to live life. Our money personalities can play a big role in that. For example, my wife and I experienced friction in our relationship due to our different money personalities, but once we identified and understood them, we resolved the issue. Taking an assessment from the Money Couple (https://5moneypersonalities.com/) helped us discover our money personalities.

I'm a Risk-Taker and Flyer, meaning I enjoy taking risks and seeing money as a tool to create and build things. My wife believed she was a Security-Seeker and Saver. However, after taking the test with me, we realized she matched as a Security-Seeker and Risk-Taker. Knowing our money personalities has helped us communicate better and work together to achieve our financial goals without conflict.

As a successful investor, I know there is no one-size-fits-all approach to personal finance. Each person has a unique money personality that influences their financial decisions. For example, spendthrifts must focus on creating a budget emphasizing savings, while Savers must find opportunities to invest their money for maximum returns. Identifying your money personality type will determine your financial decisions, whether you are a Risk-Taker or a Security-Seeker.

I am passionate about helping others achieve their financial goals through personalized investment strategies that align with their money personalities.

As I've mentioned, understanding your money personality is essential for achieving long-term financial success and lasting impact. By taking inventory of your assets and gaining insight into your money habits and tendencies, you can identify your strengths and weaknesses and work towards positive changes.

We can guide you toward financial success by uncovering your money personality type and creating a customized financial plan to help you achieve your goals and live a fulfilling life. Together, we can take your financial journey to new heights.

As a testament to the effectiveness of our approach, let me share with you the story of Eric Snell, an investor who's become a friend. He found success through our equity-based REIT model after struggling to balance his full-time job and rentals—being both a landlord and having a full-time job.

Eric initially had hesitations about working with RADD due to the dishonest practices he had encountered elsewhere. "I was scared because I had a bad experience with a real estate training company where they stole a bunch of money from us investors," Eric says. This negative experience made him reluctant to trust another company with his investments. However, Eric knew that he couldn't achieve his investing goals alone and required help navigating the complexities of real estate investing.

"I'd been investing part-time for 15 years at that point. It would take me too long to figure it out myself," he says. "I needed to partner with a company." Eric attended multiple real estate training programs and bought several courses to learn as much as possible. Despite this, he found that many companies only talked about what "used" to work and that the instructors were no longer actively investing themselves. "They just taught it," he says.

Eric was impressed by RADD's current strategies and experience, including its tax auction trips that allowed investors to join RADD experts at auctions and purchase properties. During one of these trips, Eric realized he had chosen the right team to partner with, as they could purchase four houses in one day. As Eric says, "that was the trip I realized I had chosen the right company, the right team."

Eric has gone on to make a strategic investment by partnering with RADD, securing partial ownership of premium properties. Eric has invested in various real estate deals with RAD Diversified and tax auction investors, ranging from $5,000 to $50,000. He followed **An Investor's Important Steps:**

1. He learned and used the rules of due diligence.

2. He became educated on his chosen investment vehicle.

3. He leveraged other people's experiences.

4. He leveraged other people's work.

5. He didn't let past experiences hold him back from his own success.

Doing all this enabled Eric to focus on more profitable endeavors, ultimately leading to a more balanced life.

Reflecting on his journey, Eric says, "I let RADD take the reins of my investments, and it's been a game-changer." As someone who didn't have much trust or confidence in working with investment groups, Eric's perspective has shifted since working with RAD Diversified. "At first, I looked at mutual fund stock market investing, but it didn't pass my criteria," Eric says. "Then, I turned to real estate. While I've lost money in the past with real estate investments, I haven't lost money in quite a few years now."

Eric's mindset towards investing has changed due to investing in real estate and working on the plan. "My perspective has shifted from trying to handle everything independently to embracing opportunities and recognizing them for what they are," he says. "This change in mentality has allowed me to move from a scarcity mindset to an abundance mindset."

As Eric's experience shows, everyone has a unique relationship with money shaped by their upbringing and personal preferences. That's why our Tribe recognizes the importance of understanding an individual's money personality, which tends to remain consistent, just like their love language.

An unhealthy relationship with money can lead to financial hardships, exploitation, and victimization.

To avoid such situations, individuals should aim to cultivate a healthy relationship with money that empowers them to identify and capitalize on opportunities while making well-informed financial decisions.

Cultivating a positive relationship with money can lead to healthier relationships.

> "Cultivating a positive relationship with money can lead to healthier relationships."

Understanding one's money personality and that of others can empower individuals to take proactive action rather than being victimized by their financial circumstances. Those who struggle with codependency and an unhealthy relationship with money often experience financial instability and exploitation. Therefore, developing a healthy relationship with money is crucial to avoid being taken advantage of and achieve success.

Avoiding financial loss is equally as important as making financial gains. A healthy relationship with money protects you from poor decision-making.

CAUTION–Avoid these **Ten Costly Mistakes**:

1. Rushing to make decisions.

2. Being pressured into financial decisions.

3. Relying on unreliable sources (friends, news,

self-proclaimed professionals) without performing due diligence (RADD Keys Chapter 5).

4. Investing in something they don't understand without education.

5. Investing in private unreported companies.

6. Investing in a vehicle without disclosed tangible assets.

7. Deciding they have to make a decision for short-term gain.

8. Allowing money to burn a hole in their pocket.

9. Making a greed-based decision.

10. Not considering inflation or other variables that could affect the investment.

Investing can be difficult, especially when avoiding common mistakes. By creating a matrix for each investment decision, you may be able to prevent yourself from making two of the biggest mistakes: holding onto an investment that is losing money or continuing to invest in something that isn't returning anything. While there are good investments out there, be sure to proceed with caution.

Discovering my money personality was the key to unlocking financial success.

My journey toward financial success taught me the importance of self-discovery and its role in creating a better future for yourself and your loved ones. By identifying my money personality as a Risk-Taker, I could channel my energy into smart investments to grow my wealth and create a more stable financial future.

Our Tribe member Eric sought security with his money, but he has learned to adapt. Now freed from the "Money Shackles" of his previous thinking, Eric feels liberated. "As I've seen my investments grow over the years," Eric says, "I feel a lot less stressed about money. In the past, my mindset was very controlling and focused on scarcity, but now I've learned to release control and let things be as they should. I used to worry about every penny, but I've let go of that over the years. It's a lot less stressful to have an abundance mindset and trust that everything will be okay. There will always be plenty of investment opportunities."

Eric's transformation as a Security-Seeker with a more abundance-minded investor exemplifies how understanding your money personality can lead to financial success.

Another way to leverage your money personality is to align your financial decisions with your values.

When you make choices that align with your core beliefs, you're more likely to feel satisfied and fulfilled with your financial situation. For example, if you value experiences over possessions, you might spend money on travel instead of buying a new car.

The way you make financial decisions can have a huge impact on your life. Research has shown that aligning your financial decisions with your values can lead to greater happiness, satisfaction, and control over your life.

- The Journal of Financial Therapy study found that people who felt good about their finances were likelier to have habits aligned with their values.[18]

- A Charles Schwab study suggests those who had thought

---

18   Archuleta, KL and Dale, A. 2016. *Money and happiness: A review of the literature.* Retrieved from Journal of Finance Therapy, 7 (2), 1-21.

about what they wanted to do with their money were more likely to report feeling financially stable.[19]

- A study published in the Journal of Consumer Psychology found that people who made financial decisions based on what was important to them reported higher levels of happiness and satisfaction than those who did not.[20] These statistics suggest that aligning your financial decisions with your values can positively impact your well-being.

Understanding your money personality is an important step towards achieving financial stability and success. It will enable you to make informed financial decisions that align with your values and goals. Once again, the five money personalities are: *Spenders, Flyers, Security-Seekers, Savers, and Risk-Takers.*

Knowing your tendencies will help you create a financial plan that aligns with your goals. You can determine your money personality by tracking your spending habits or taking a money personality test. Aligning your financial decisions with your values can lead to greater happiness, satisfaction, and control over your life.

Finding a team or partner that aligns with your values and goals can also help you leverage your money personality. It is important to proceed cautiously in investing while avoiding the Ten Costly Mistakes and making smart investments by creating a matrix for each investment decision.

---

19   n/d. 2019. *FOMO fuels American spending.* Retrieved from https://www.aboutschwab.com/modernwealth2019.

20   Kim, MS and Johnson, KKP. 2016. *Making spending decisions that promote happiness: How being mindful, committed, and autonomous can make a difference.* Retrieved from Journal of Consumer Psychology, 26 (4), 547-557.

Chapter Review

> If you'd like to practice what you've learned in this chapter, I invite you to check out the exercises at this link:
> https://therad.com/moneyshackles/workbook

The chapter exercises encourage you to reflect on your money personality, strategize how to attain your financial goals by including tactics that use your personalities' strengths, and identify any negative beliefs or habits that may hinder your financial success.

1. By understanding your relationship with money, you can take control of your financial decisions and move towards a more stable future. This includes reviewing:

    *   The ***Five Money Personalities*** is a tool to help understand financial behaviors, attitudes, and habits.

    *   ***An Investor's Important Steps*** allows you to focus on more profitable endeavors, ultimately leading to a more balanced life.

    *   The ***Ten Costly Mistakes*** are a tool to help evaluate and combat poor decision-making with investments.

2. By identifying your unique tendencies, you can work towards positive changes and create a customized financial plan that aligns with your goals. A personalized investment strategy, leveraging experts' experiences and work, and shifting perspectives will help guide to financial success.

3. To avoid financial hardships and victimization, you should cultivate a healthy relationship with money that empowers you to identify opportunities and make informed

decisions. This includes understanding your money personality and aligning your financial decisions with your values and goals while avoiding common mistakes and making smart investments.

How does your relationship with money affect your financial decision-making? Your money personality influences your financial decisions and behaviors, leading to financial stability and success or financial instability and failure. Understanding and cultivating a healthy relationship with money is essential for achieving long-term financial goals and a fulfilling life.

CHAPTER 4

REFRAMING DEBT AND BORROWING

What is debt? What does your debt look like?

The concept of debt is familiar to most people, but it can also produce a feeling of stress and worry. This comes with the inability to make payments and the limitations that debt can place on your life. It affects your budget and the lifestyle you want to live, whether it's buying a home, starting a business, or simply taking a vacation.

- The average American household carries around $169,242 in debt,[21] according to recent studies.

- Credit card debt, student loans, and mortgages are the most significant sources of debt for most individuals.

- Soaring interest rates on credit cards, student loans, and other sources of debt to cover necessities can make it challenging to pay off the debt, leading to stress and anxiety.

---

21 El Issa, E. 2023. 2022 *American Household Credit Card Debt Study.* Retrieved from https://www.nerdwallet.com/article/credit-cards/average-credit-card-debt-household.

- Moreover, studies have found that people with high debt levels are more likely to experience depression, anxiety, and other mental health issues.[22]

Debt can strain relationships and harm your mental and physical health, especially if you enjoy taking risks or are impulsive. This fear can lead to poor decision-making, even for those who manage their finances carefully, such as Savers and Security-Seekers who make many sacrifices to avoid debt burden.

Meet Robin Thomas, someone extremely successful, and a force of nature I'm happy to call a friend. She was a roofing contractor without retirement savings after a difficult divorce.

"I made a good amount of money, and lived a nice life and everything," she says. "But then when I thought about the future, and [I thought about] when would I be able to retire? Because you can't really guarantee it. Social Security is going to be there, but is it even going to be enough to, you know, pay out what I'm used to living or how I'm used to living? So for me it was reinventing the fact that I started off with nothing and having to move into and learn."

At 53 years old, she had to reinvent herself and find a way to secure her future. That's when she dived deeper into alternative investing, and we met through our RAD Inner Circle. Being in a like-minded community with a wide variety of exciting investment vehicles, she expanded her education.

Robin has learned about diversifying her portfolio, utilizing borrowing strategies and IRAs to increase her potential gains, and cycling her investment returns to compound results. She has been able to watch her money grow, giving her a sense of peace and security that she never had

---

22   Fay, B. 2023. *The Emotional Effects of Debt.* Retrieved from https://www.debt.org/advice/emotional-effects/.

before. Robin's story is a reminder. No matter where you are, even if you start investing later, it's still possible.

It's important to harness your money to make it work for you, and debt and borrowing are one of those ways.

> "It's important to harness your money to make it work for you, and debt and borrowing are one of those ways."

Some people immediately try to get rid of their debt as fast as possible, but that's not always the best approach. You're not maximizing the return on your investment. Instead, you need to consider whether investing your money and earning a higher return are more beneficial than paying off the debt immediately. *If you can make more money by investing the money and then cycle it through investments to pay off the debt and continue to invest, you have the money that makes a higher return. It's crucial to maximize the return on your investment and use the debt to your advantage.*

Have you considered the impact these methods have on your financial health? If you're like many people, managing money might not come naturally. It certainly didn't for me, especially growing up in a financially unstable environment. Even as an adult with a decent income, I still struggled to comprehend how to make my money work. I lacked the knowledge and skills to invest, buy a house, or keep my car from being repossessed.

It can become your worst enemy if you don't have a responsible and healthy relationship with money. It's essential to understand the consequences of debt and take control of your finances to avoid getting stuck in a perpetual cycle of survival. Learning to use your money effectively is vital to achieving financial success.

But what if you could break free from the cycle of debt and stress? What if you could achieve the stability, comfort, lifestyle, and legacy you've always dreamed of?

It's possible but requires a different approach than the status quo.

It means being intentional with your finances and making strategic choices that align with your long-term goals and values. It means seeking education and resources to help you make informed decisions and take control of your financial future.

If you're looking to improve your financial literacy and take control of your finances, there are many resources available to you. You can find valuable Personal Finance Information (budgeting, investing, and debt management) through:

- Books
    - "The Richest Man in Babylon" by George S. Clason
    - "Rich Dad Poor Dad" by Robert Kiyosaki
    - "Good Debt, Bad Debt: Knowing the Difference Can Save Your Financial Life" by Jon Hanson
    - "The Alternative Answer: The Nontraditional Investments That Drive the World's Best-Performing Portfolios" by Bob Rice
    - "Debt Millionaire: Most People Will Never Build Real Wealth, But Not You" by Brandon Withrow

"While it's important to pay off debts and manage your budget wisely, don't forget that time is of the essence when it comes to achieving your dreams."

- Courses
    - Coursera (https://www.coursera.org/)
    - edX (https://www.edx.org/)
    - Khan Academy (https://www.khanacademy.org/)
    - LinkedIn Learning (https://www.linkedin.com/learning/)
    - Udemy (https://www.udemy.com/)
- Online Resources
    - FINRA (https://www.finra.org/)

- ◦ Investopedia (https://www.investopedia.com/)
- ◦ Morningstar (https://www.morningstar.com/)
- ◦ The Motley Fool (https://www.fool.com/)
- ◦ NerdWallet (https://www.nerdwallet.com/)

However, not all resources are created equal, and it's important to choose those that are reputable and effective. Most importantly, resources that resonate with you and your preferences. Researching and comparing different options can help you find the best resources for your needs and goals. It's also essential to remember that no resource can replace the benefits of seeking guidance from successful financial experts and committing to your financial plan.

You can create a life of abundance and impact and leave a lasting legacy that reflects the values and priorities you hold most dear.

I will expand on this concept and be real with you.

If you want to achieve a certain lifestyle, you must separate it from your debt.

If the debt is going to your lifestyle, if you're building up a lifestyle that doesn't work for you right now between the quadrants of the Freedom Chart in Chapter 1, then it's coun-

> "If you want to achieve a certain lifestyle, you must separate it from your debt."

terproductive to your mobility of freedom and an unproductive utilization of money.

Your debt can work for or against you by expanding your investments or becoming a liability. Understanding how to acquire more capital and make your money work for you is essential. If you have a significant amount of debt, it's a different conversation, but when starting with little, you need to take it slow and utilize your resources to their full potential.

The American Dream is achievable, but it's different at every stage of life, and you need to be realistic about what you can achieve in a certain amount of time. Waiting forty years to live your dream isn't the best approach, and you need to start building it as soon as possible to make the most of your life. If you want to live life and live your dream, you don't want to miss forty years just to save to be debt-free and start investing later. Simultaneously, if you start later in life like Robin, you can still succeed.

As an investor, you must make the right moves and choose the right investments to achieve your goals. Several business owners and entrepreneurs have had mishaps in their pasts but have turned it around to make their money work. Ray Kroc, with acquiring McDonald's, Richard Branson and launching Virgin Atlantic, or even Oprah Winfrey and her OWN Network, have utilized debt to leverage investments and become some of the wealthiest individuals in recent history. Their use of debt to build portfolios and secure financial futures is a strategy to learn from, where you identify what are the right moves and what is the right investment.

Learn from the past, but not at the expense of the present or future.

While it's important to pay off debts and manage your budget wisely, don't forget that time is of the essence when it comes to achieving your dreams.

You're told to pay your debts first and worry about your credit score, and if you don't, it can have financial implications, affecting your ability to obtain a car or house. Going through those hoops, you know about budgeting, the several rules of savings like having an account for emergencies and another for big purchase savings, which can be seen as similar to the money buckets.

There are several popular methods for managing your budget and paying off debts.

1. You may have heard of the 50/30/20 and 70/20/10 rules, which suggest allocating percentages of your income toward spending, savings, and debt payments.

2. Another popular method is the Snowball Method, where you pay off your debts from smallest to largest balance regardless of interest rate, using the paid-off amount to add to the next debt's payment, thus building momentum.

3. Alternatively, the Avalanche Method focuses on paying off debts with the highest interest rate first, regardless of balance, potentially saving you thousands in interest payments.

"Why should you wait until you're debt-free to start investing? Forget everything you learned about how to take care of debt. Why create more limitations when there's no need?"

All of these methods advise once you're debt-free, you're to continue to avoid debt and focus on investing for the future, which always comes at a much later date. I believe by shifting your focus from these stereotypical methods, you can actually accelerate your journey toward financial freedom.

It is important to understand the history and concepts related to debt.

The Colonial era viewed personal private debt and borrowing differently from the present day. Money, too, was perceived differently, with the era emphasizing the value of goods in transactions over cash or coin exchange due to a money shortage and mercantilist economics.

Credit was not readily available, and borrowing was typically reserved for the wealthy or businesses, including farms, especially to finance trade. It was often secured with collateral instead of tracking debt.[23]

During the Industrial era, the availability of credit expanded, and borrowing became more common, fueled by the growth of the banking system. The emergence of new forms of credit made it easier for

23   Olegario, R. 2019. *The History of Credit in America*. Retrieved from https://oxfordre.com/americanhistory/display/10.1093/acrefore/9780199329175.001.0001/acrefore-9780199329175-e-625;jsessionid=45494381101264866C694B4F9B220832.

people outside the wealthy classes to buy goods and services. It became stigmatized as a sign of financial irresponsibility or lack of self-control, particularly in the years leading up to the Great Depression.

Does this sound familiar with today's rhetoric?

Let's consider further how we define those terms today:

- *Debt* refers to the money and resources that one owes to another person or entity, such as loans, credit card balances, mortgages, and lines of credit.

- *Borrowing* is obtaining money or resources to pay it back with interest or fees.

However, the truth is that borrowing comes with inherent risks, particularly if you default on a loan or have high debt levels. Depending on your financial situation and your debt type, it can be considered a high-risk or low-risk investment. For example, payday loans and credit card debts are often high-risk, while personal loans, mortgages, and student loans are generally considered lower risk.

This was something I really didn't understand when I was younger. I have since learned it can benefit me and others.

The traditional concept of debt and borrowing can be a valuable benefit. It's not a vehicle of consumerism or something to be ashamed of using that you must fix immediately. Redefine not only how you value money and investing but the paths you can take to get there, and debt and borrowing are some of the most powerful tools in your arsenal.

Why should you wait until you're debt-free to start investing? Forget everything you learned about how to take care of debt. Why create more limitations when there's no need?

Utilizing credit cards for short-term financing to purchase alternative investments can be risky, especially if the interest rates are high or the investment doesn't perform as expected. However, you can see greater potential for financial freedom by doing thorough due diligence and investing in a wide range of alternative investments.

Some Tribe members have found success by cycling their credit cards as part of a long-term investment strategy, which we will discuss further. *The key to making this strategy work is to cycle money through multiple investments to achieve greater compound returns and make your money work for you in achieving your Real American Dream. You could become the lender instead of only being the borrower.*

Did I set off alarm bells? I'll be setting off a few more before I finish.

If you surrender to my method, your view of finances will change.

I can tell you that this may be one of the hardest changes you will make.

You're not just learning new things. You're rewiring your brain and shifting it into a new perspective. You're taking an **Alternative Approach to Debt.** It will take time to break habits, but when you do, you will look at debt, financial education, and investing differently.

The role of debt and borrowing to achieve your financial goals is simple: put the money to work over 90% of the time to generate more capital to add to your income, and don't buy big purchases or frivolous things all the time. Does it happen? Absolutely—which is where I figure the 10% comes in.

These are flexible and arbitrary numbers, so create percentages that work best for you if your debt and borrowing balances are the overwhelming majority towards investments.

Remember, if you're going into debt with a loan or credit card for university, trade, or financial education, do it. That's an investment for your growth, personal development, and ability to change your financial future. DO NOT USE DEBT FOR LIFESTYLE.

I will reiterate.

Debt is a crucial aspect of personal finance that can significantly affect our mental, physical, and financial health.

I didn't know in my twenties that the traditional approach to debt management could limit my ability to generate wealth and take years, if not decades, to achieve financial freedom. It took time to change my perspective and methodology to use debt as a tool to put my money to work and create the life I deserve.

The traditional approach to debt management focuses on paying off debt and then investing for the future. Instead, we should view debt and borrowing as tools to put our money to work and generate more capital, as long as most of our debt is directed towards investments. While changing our perspective on debt and borrowing may be challenging, achieving financial freedom and creating the life we deserve is necessary.

"It feels satisfying," is Robin's assessment of seeing a portfolio grow. She would agree with many of the assessments and strategies that could help expand your investment potential. "The idea that you can get into the deal, watch the deal as it progresses, and understand what the costs truly are....It's a really good feeling....You don't want to wait and be in the position that I was in, because you are going to be a lot better off." You simply have to start now.

Have you ever considered this alternative method's benefits in putting your money to work and how it can positively impact your financial health and help you achieve your dreams?

It's about earning a small return on your investment and compounding that return over time. Say I take out a $10,000 personal loan with an interest rate of 8% per year, and I use that money to invest in the stock market or a mutual fund with an average return of 10% per year.

In the first year, I would pay $800 in interest on the loan and earn $1,000 in investment returns, leaving me with a net gain of $200. However, in the second year, I would not only earn a return on my original investment but also on the $200 that was earned in the first year, and so on.

The difference might not seem like much at first, but the compounding effect of the investment can add up to significant capital growth.

It's not just about the numbers, either.

Investing can change your relationship with money and your entire mindset. It's about shifting your consciousness and becoming an investor rather than just someone who saves a little bit here and there. This shift can be challenging, as it requires reframing your mind and even changing the vibrational energy within your body.

But the benefits are enormous. As you invest and see your money grow, you'll attract more abundance and better relationships. It's not just about the financial returns but about **Two Wealth Mindsets:**

1.   "The Power of Attraction" is a force that brings you exactly what you focus on. This means that if you're fixated on negative thoughts or bad things happening to you, that's exactly what you will attract. But if you focus on your goals, dreams, and ambitions with a laser-like intensity, you'll attract

opportunities, people, and resources to help you achieve them.

2. "The Law of Abundance" is a universal law that states that there is an infinite amount of resources available to everyone and that abundance is our birthright. This means there is more than enough money, wealth, and success for everyone. The key is to believe in yourself, take massive action, and tap into the abundance surrounding us all. By adopting an abundance mindset, you can create limitless opportunities for yourself and achieve anything you want.

The American Dream has evolved over time, as discussed in Chapter 1, and so have our perspectives, relationships, and education with money. Acknowledging the impact of borrowing and the inherent risk of debt is crucial. Embrace these concepts, and don't think about investing as a way to make a little extra cash. Think about it as a way to transform your life and become more empowered and confident.

Again, the benefits of cycling money through more investments include potentially higher returns, greater financial security, and the ability to achieve your American Dream. Whether that's retiring comfortably, starting a business, or leaving a lasting legacy for future generations. Using tools like compound interest can help your money grow exponentially over time, providing even greater financial freedom and opportunities.

Consider how this affects your options from the Financial Decision Tree based on money personalities and buckets focused on investment risks with all the benefits it brings. For example:

*   The "Spender Money Personality" can benefit from implementing three strategies: setting a budget, auto-mating savings, and investing in experiences. Creating

a budget can help prioritize spending and redirect
funds towards saving and investing while automating
savings can ensure consistent savings without much
effort. Investing in experiences can also provide more
fulfillment than material possessions. As a Spender, they
may be comfortable with higher-risk investments for
potentially higher returns, but having a solid emergency
fund is important. These strategies can help you enjoy
the money while achieving financial goals and building
wealth.

• The "Flyer Money Personality" looks for investment
strategies with potentially high returns. Alternative options
include investing in real estate, art or collectibles, and
peer-to-peer lending platforms. Real estate can offer steady
rental income and appreciation over time. Investing in
art or collectibles can provide significant returns if the
asset's value increases. Peer-to-peer lending platforms allow
investors to lend money to individuals or businesses and
earn interest on the loans, potentially higher returns than
traditional fixed-income investments. These alternative
strategies still carry risk but may be better for those seeking
potentially high returns without the volatility of individual
stocks and options. Flyers hate money drama and must
monitor their investments.

• The "Security-Seeker Money Personality" tends to invest
in low-risk assets such as dividend-paying stocks with a
strong track record of stability and REITs to diversify their
portfolio to reduce risk. They also prioritize building an
emergency fund to cover unexpected expenses. Regarding
risk buckets, they prefer low-risk or conservative investments such as stocks, REITs, and money market accounts
insured by the Federal Deposit Insurance Corporation

(FDIC), while avoiding high-risk investments such as alternative venture funds. The benefits of this approach include a lower risk of losing money, steady and reliable income from investments, peace of mind, and reduced anxiety about market fluctuations. Security-Seekers need to balance high return investment risk too.

- The "Saver Money Personality" can benefit from diversifying their investments, considering a side hustle, and avoiding analysis paralysis. They may prefer low-risk investments, but it's important to consider higher-risk investments to potentially earn higher returns over the long term. By following these strategies, Savers can build wealth while maintaining their savings habits and potentially increase their returns.

- For a "Risk-Taker Money Personality," three main investment strategies include investing in high-growth alternative investments, venture funds, and even cryptocurrency. These strategies can offer a high potential for returns but have higher risks. Risk-Takers may invest in aggressive growth, speculative, or alternative risk buckets. Benefits of being a Risk-Taker include the potential for high returns, excitement, and diversification of their portfolio, which can balance the risk of more conservative investments and potentially lead to greater overall returns. Risk-Takers should always carefully consider worst case scenarios and create safety backstops as a part of their decisions.

Investing is the key to achieving financial freedom and unlocking the power of abundance. By understanding the impact of debt and shifting our mindset, we can secure our financial future and achieve our wildest dreams.

We all have unique money personalities and risk tolerances that can help us personalize our investment strategies to match our priorities. It's important to remember that investing isn't just about the numbers but also about attracting abundance with a positive mindset. So, let's focus on building wealth and attracting opportunities by cultivating an abundance mindset. However, investing is a long-term game, and success requires discipline, patience, and a big-picture perspective.

Investing comes with risks, but remember the potential rewards like *compounding returns, diversification, and building a portfolio that aligns with our values and goals.* We can set ourselves up for a prosperous and fulfilling financial future by educating ourselves, seeking expert guidance, and sticking to our financial plans.

Chapter Review

If you'd like to practice what you've learned
in this chapter, I invite you to check out the
exercises at this link:
https://therad.com/moneyshackles/workbook

The chapter exercises encourage you to look at your own changing attitudes towards debt and borrowing over time, identify the resources and strategies that best fit your needs, and discuss the compounding effect on your capital growth and financial freedom.

1. A brief overview of the history and evolution of debt and borrowing highlights the changing perceptions and attitudes toward it. It also emphasizes the importance of redefining how we value money and investing and how debt and borrowing can be powerful tools to achieve financial goals.

2. The impact debt can have on your financial, mental, and physical health, relationships, and lifestyle can be invasive or a tool. You are introduced to the concept of reinvention and successfully managing finances. Many resources are available to improve your financial literacy:

    •   Utilizing budgeting and savings strategies that solely focus on being debt free may not be the most effective or robust strategy if you're distracted from the potential rewards making investments could bring.

    •   *Personal Finance Information* on budgeting, investing, and debt management can be found through the right books, courses, and online resources.

    •   If you are willing to adopt a new perspective on debt and borrowing, like the *Alternative Approach to Debt*, it can positively impact your financial health and help you achieve your dreams. Rather than viewing debt as a burden, use it as a tool to generate more capital for investments. By investing, you can change your mindset and attract more abundance and better relationships. The compounding effect of investing can add up to significant capital growth, which provides greater financial freedom and opportunities.

3.   Embrace the *Two Wealth Mindsets* to change your perspective on money and scale the power of your financial abundance. With the "Power of Attraction" and the "Law of Abundance," you can attract opportunities and tap into unlimited resources. Especially if you aim to understand your money personality and risk tolerance to tailor your investment strategies.

What is debt? What does your debt look like? Debt is the amount of borrowed money that needs to be paid back with interest. It can significantly impact one's financial, mental, and physical health, relationships, and lifestyle. Adopting a new perspective on debt and investing can be used as a tool to generate more capital for investments and achieve financial goals.

CHAPTER 5

GETTING STARTED WITH ALTERNATIVE INVESTING

How do you begin your quest for financial freedom?

Investing can be challenging or confusing for anyone. More so for the stock market's ups and downs. Remember, you can budget utilizing money buckets and risk buckets.

This is one of many "Money Shackles" created by an old, unbalanced system. Building wealth doesn't have to be beyond your reach.

As you know, on my journey to financial freedom, I had trouble figuring out how to achieve the success I sought after that cold New Year's night. After a time of reinventing myself, I reached out to some successful people and learned from them. After applying their advice, I became a top-performing headhunter, as I've mentioned.

Then I soon realized that consulting wasn't giving me the personal and professional fulfillment I needed. So, I decided to start my own company instead. With this new venture, I gained valuable experience. I made more money but my money wasn't being put to work yet.

But not everyone was on board with what I was doing. Some people made promises they couldn't keep or tried to take advantage of me in ways that weren't fair. Exploring different tactical options and working hard daily, I figured out how to make my money grow reliably.

Now that my journey has taken me this far, I'm excited to share these insights with you.

The journey toward financial success begins by understanding that there are alternative paths to the traditional system.

The traditional system has created "Money Shackles." It limits the freedom of Americans. Don't be discouraged by the exclusivity of certain investments or the confusion that can come with them. Instead, focus on finding alternative investments that align with your passions and goals.

Alternative investments offer a way to diversify your portfolio across a broader range of risks and rewards. These opportunities do not fall within the traditional forms of investing like the stock market, bonds, or mutual funds. Many traditional investments come with high barriers to entry, and the system often favors certain individuals over others, making it difficult to participate and succeed.

Alternative investments include:

- Real Estate Investment Trusts (REITs), Farms and Ranches, or Vacation Rentals
- Precious Gems and Metals, Oil and Gas Partnerships, or Timberland
- Vintage Cars, Rare Books, or Historical and Entertainment Memorabilia
- Angel Investing, Growth Equity, or Leveraged Buyouts (LBOs)

- Renewable Energy Projects, Transportation, or Data Centers
- Patents, Software, or Media and Video Game Rights
- Medical or Equipment Financing, Small Business Loans, or Social Impact Bonds

Then, in 2012, everything changed. The **Jumpstart Our Business Startups (JOBS) Act**[24] made alternative investments accessible to accredited and to non-accredited investors, leveling the playing field and allowing everyone to invest and profit from their investments. It led to a distinction between Regulation A+ funds, and Regulation D funds. Regulation A+ is open to accredited and non-accredited investors, while the long-standing Regulation D is simply open to accredited investors. The act extended the concept of fractionalized ownership to the "everyday" American. It is an incredible tool to partially own businesses, real estate, ventures, farms, and more without having to do the work.

The JOBS Act has been a game-changer for Americans and new investors looking to build and find their financial freedom. Investing in small businesses, startups, and other private companies makes it easier. Before, investing in these types of companies was only available to a small group of wealthy individuals and institutions. Since 2012, the JOBS Act has led to a democratization of investing, where everyone can participate. A few of the benefits include:

- The creation of crowdfunding platforms, which provides much-needed capital to smaller businesses and opportunities for everyday Americans to support those they believe in.
- Companies can use social media and online advertising to promote investment opportunities to reach a wider audience.

------

24   n/d. 2012 (2023). *Spotlight on Jumpstart Our Business Startups (JOBS) Act.* Retrieved from https://www.sec.gov/spotlight/jobs-act

- Creating a new category of regulated securities offerings known as Regulation A+, allowing non-accredited investors in the securities space for the first time.

The rise of Regulation A+ crowdfunding has been one of the most notable changes, with over $211 million raised in 2020 and projections to grow to $200 billion in 2025.[25] That's not all. Even Regulation D funding has seen a massive increase, with over $331 billion raised between 2021-2022. This has been due to the policy allowing additional sectors that could apply with the SEC.[26] Companies can now raise up to $75 million annually through Regulation A+, which has seen over $1.8 billion raised in 2022 and alleviated many businesses trying to acquire financing.

Similarly to REITs, Angel Investing, and the varying Small Business types of investments (from loans to crowdfunding), Growth Equity,[27] Medical and Equipment Financing, and Social Impact Bonds have seen an increase in potential investment opportunities and capital.

The JOBS Act has given Americans the power to build their dreams, and it's showing in the shift toward alternative investments. As more people seek to control their investment decisions, traditional stock investments are not the only option.

25   Arora, K. 2021. *The Meteoric Rise of Equity Crowdfunding.* Retrieved from https://www.forbes.com/sites/forbesagencycouncil/2021/12/20/the-meteoric-rise-of-equity-crowdfunding/?sh=762b140a4d41.

26   Alois, JD. 2023. *Investment Crowdfunding: Reg A+ and Reg D Data.* Retrieved from https://www.crowdfundinsider.com/2023/02/202101-investment-crowdfunding-reg-a-and-reg-d-data/.

27   Arel, J, et al. 2012. *The JOBS Act: A Game Changer For Emerging Growth Companies.* Retrieved from https://www.mondaq.com/unitedstates/corporate-and-company-law/171726/the-jobs-act-a-game-changer-for-emerging-growth-companies.

This is what alternative investments offer: a way to diversify your portfolio and potentially achieve your dreams.

There are various alternative investments, such as peer-to-peer lending, real estate, art, collectibles, private equity, and more. It's essential to research and assess the credibility of the companies you're investing in. Working with experienced professionals can be a great way to ensure your investments are successful.

It's time to break free from the traditional system and create your path to financial success with the right knowledge, education, and alternative investments. You can achieve financial freedom and long-term success by taking calculated risks and seeking opportunities that align with your values and goals.

That's why choosing the right companies and understanding the key to success is important.

It's crucial to do your due diligence and assess the credibility of the companies you're investing in. This helps you gain a better understanding of their operations and financial health. By doing so, you can make informed decisions and increase your chances of achieving higher capital returns over time and with the practice of understanding the finer points of becoming an investor.

The RADD Keys give you the tools for investing in the right companies:

1. Understand the founder's story and find a successful track record.

2. Invest in real businesses, not just good ideas.

3. Is it clear whether the business offers a real product?

4. What is the business model for profitability?

5. Does the business have existing revenue?

6. Do they know their current profit margins per product?

7. Is there a specific, measurable timeline for the company's growth?

8. Does business exist in regulated industries?

9. What are the biggest obstacles to success? Does the business have a plan for overcoming obstacles?

10. What type of impact does the business have in the world?

A remarkable friend, Corinthia Davis, once expressed a sentiment that all Americans can believe in to some extent, "I like to keep making money to have more money to invest…The key is to one day not have to work."

How does she do it?

Well, she's not afraid to take action when it comes to investing. Especially when she's confident in the vehicle, like real estate alternatives.

She's no stranger to the real estate game, after all. Corinthia has a head start thanks to her father's influence from a young age.

But it's not just about knowing the industry. It's about having integrity and doing her due diligence with companies. Where did she learn these values? From her father of course, a retired policeman who instilled in her basic financial skills, like the importance of being self-sufficient and managing resources. He also taught her the value of cycling money to generate wealth.

Corinthia takes these lessons seriously. She doesn't just stop at the basics. She continues to expand her education and knowledge to build her legacy one step at a time. With each new investment, she's growing her portfolio and securing her future. Right towards her goal of not having to work.

Alternative investments can offer great long-term opportunities for growth.

Due diligence is not the only key.

It's important to research, work with experienced professionals, and be transparent about your agendas. As you gain more knowledge and education, you'll feel less risk and more confidence in your investments. From understanding your dreams and money relationships to varying financial strategies, there are options for everyone when you **Develop an Alternative Mindset.**

When I was younger, I asked the smartest, wealthiest man I knew about his best books for developing wealth. He suggested "The Richest Man in Babylon,"[28] by George Clason. I read it for the first time during a plane trip.

It is a collection of overlapping themes set in ancient Babylon, providing valuable personal finance and wealth-building advice. Three parables, seven concepts, and five steps, in fact.

Using the book's strategies can help build wealth. It highlights personal development, setting future plans, and protecting wealth. Everything I dive into is also a little more accessible to contemporary audiences. For example, Shaquille O'Neal taught me a lesson on controlling lifestyle and alternative investments as recently as five years ago.

I watched a video[29] where he took a sheet of paper and ripped it in half. He demonstrated that you should put 50% of your income into savings, don't touch it, and then he ripped the sheet of paper in half again. Now save this 25%, ideally for investments. The remaining 25% of your income is what you should live on. To be fair, if you're living on

---

28   Clason, GS. 1926. *The Richest Man in Babylon.* Penguin Books.

29   CNBS Make It. 2018. *Shaquille O'Neal's Money Advice To Young People.* Retrieved from https://www.youtube.com/watch?v=D4RppC6PHZU.

$30,000 a year, this may not be possible compared to someone living on $1,500,000 a year. However, there's one minor detail that remains.

Your lifestyle costs should not exceed your income. A portion of your money should be going towards savings. Or, as I would say, investments.

It simply requires controlling your lifestyle and putting as much money to work as possible. To compound those returns, and eventually, it will help change your living situations and legacy.

For example, Corinthia, a successful business owner, is driven to achieve financial independence and create a lifestyle that allows her to focus on the things she loves. Playing tennis and doing yoga. But she knew that to make her money work for her, she needed to invest smartly. Not a get-rich-quick-scheme, but something with cash flow.

When building wealth, it is important to focus on earning a high income and managing your cash flow. Without careful management, you could find yourself in extremely frivolous debt or without your money working for you. The "Cashflow" game[30] helps bridge O'Neal's explanation of investing and can help by teaching you how to reduce expenses and increase cash flow with alternative sources of income. The goal is to cover your monthly expenses by passive income from investments, at which point you will break the "Money Shackles." This approach involves creating multiple streams of income that exceed expenses, allowing you to build wealth and create the life you desire.

This is what Corinthia has done. To take calculated risks, do her due diligence, and consider the options that help her generate the best rewards to create a life she loves. By following these principles, Corinthia has not only built a successful investment portfolio but also found a sense of purpose.

---

30   n/d. 1996 (2023). *Cashflow*. Retrieved from https://store.richdad.com/?gclid=CjwKCA-jwuqiiBlhBtEiwATgvIxDM1b--fJg7zoqnFmkb/PuLvIs1e1B1atAYCSMehESu9_qTOPX-so7xoCgmsQAvD_BwE.

At the end of the day, that is what it is about. A purpose aligning with your values.

Stay true to it and pursue investments that not only generate financial returns but also have a positive impact on society. Imagine the power of giving back and community building as you make your investment decisions. Trust me, I know it works because I've only found success when my purpose is the goal of investing. Even my business partner Amy always speaks about it. She constantly discusses and redefines her "WHY," and encourages others to question what theirs is too.

As you build your wealth with alternative investments, plan for the future, dedicate your resources, and create a lasting legacy that transcends monetary gain. Your impact can be transformative, leaving a mark beyond your lifetime.

Just commit to it.

Chapter Review

> If you'd like to practice what you've learned in this chapter, I invite you to check out the exercises at this link:
> https://therad.com/moneyshackles/workbook

The chapter exercises encourage you to identify different alternative investment vehicles, apply the RADD Keys and research their credibility and risks. Then, discuss how these vehicles could or could not be implemented by reflecting on your goals.

1.   *The JOBS Act* has made alternative investments accessible to all, creating a more level playing field. This has opened up new opportunities for everyday Americans to achieve their financial dreams with:

    •   Optional reading "The Richest Man in Babylon" for starting your education on wealth building.

    •   Alternative investments offer diversification and long-term growth opportunities.

    •   Reflecting on desires, values, and goals again and how they apply to alternative investment vehicles.

2.   It's important to research and assess the credibility of the companies you're investing in using *The RAD Keys*. These keys are a due diligence tool to help minimize risk effects when investing.

3.   When considering alternative investments, don't forget to work with experienced professionals and be transparent about your agendas. By following the principles of *Developing an Alternative Mindset*, such

as controlling your lifestyle costs and investing wisely,
you can build wealth, achieve financial freedom, and
leave a lasting legacy that aligns with your values.

How do you begin your quest for financial freedom? To begin
your quest for financial freedom, start by educating yourself, reflecting
on your values, and strategizing for the best investment vehicles.
Consider alternative investments as a way to diversify and achieve long-
term growth, but make sure to do your due diligence and work with
experienced professionals.

CHAPTER 6

CHOOSING FRACTIONAL OWNERSHIP

Can owning alternative investments be the right step toward your dreams?

Many people, maybe yourself included, have the same desire to invest, own a business, and have money work for them. However, there's a reliance on the traditional investing routes because they're familiar. Then a belief starts permeating people when several **Obstacles Preventing Investing,** like:

1. Insufficient funds to invest in a business or real estate.

2. May not have the time, energy, or knowledge to operate and manage a business or real estate property.

3. Turning to financial planners, who may not have the necessary experience or knowledge to provide effective guidance.

This is part of the perception from the traditional exclusive and high

barrier to entry. It's a never ending "Freedom Trap" that has systemati-
cally gotten tighter and tighter.

What if I told you there are keys to unlocking your "Money Shackles."

Are you tired of the same old investment strategies that have been
around for ages?

Have you ever considered fractional ownership and other alternative
investment options that might be the key to achieving your American
Dream?

What if you could become a Fractional Leader?

Before we dive deeper, let's reiterate a few definitions:

- Investing is the act of putting your money into assets to
  generate a return. These assets can come in different forms,
  such as traditional stocks, alternative real estate, etc. By
  investing, you're essentially putting your money to work for
  you, to generate passive income.

- Alternative investing refers to investing in assets that are not
  traditional stocks, bonds, or cash investments. These alternative assets include real estate, private equity, commodities, art,
  and other non-traditional business investment opportunities.
  One way to participate in alternative investing is through
  fractional ownership.

- Fractional ownership allows investors to own a portion of an
  asset rather than the entire asset. This approach to investing
  provides individuals with access to assets previously only available to institutional investors or high-net-worth individuals.
  By investing in alternative assets through fractional ownership,
  investors can diversify their portfolios and seek higher returns.

Building a portfolio of investments is crucial to achieving financial
freedom. A well-diversified portfolio can help you minimize risk and
maximize returns. With so many investment options out there, it can
be overwhelming to know where to start.

Kevin Mantell, a great friend, shared his journey of how he reinvented himself and achieved financial freedom through alternative investing and fractional ownership in Chapter 2. He's a rockstar in discovering new ways to make money.

He invested in high-value assets previously out of reach, and he's been able to benefit from property appreciation and rental income without the hassle of being a landlord. It's his philosophy. "There's opportunities everywhere. . . I've moved money from my traditional 401(k)s, which was an IRA, and then moved it to a self-directed IRA… allows me the flexibility to give direction of where I want my investments, instead of just a traditional stock or bond market."

If you're looking to build a well-diversified portfolio and minimize risk while maximizing returns like Kevin, do it.

Alternative investing is the key to unlocking the Redefined American Dream.

The world of alternative investments is evolving rapidly, and fractional ownership is just one example of how new approaches disrupt traditional models. You can position yourself for financial success if you break free from the "Money Shackles."

The solution is delving deeper into this investment world and reaping the benefits.

To be clear, with every investment opportunity comes risks, and fractional ownership is no exception. That's why it's important to fully understand the risks associated and take steps to mitigate them. By investigating options, you can make informed investment decisions and potentially achieve your financial goals.

Here's a **Business Checklist** covering what you've learned so far and based on The RAD Keys when analyzing the companies and people behind the investing opportunities:

- ☐ Which Risk Bucket
- ☐ Shared Beliefs
- ☐ Owners
- ☐ Past Business Experiences
- ☐ Filter Out Sob Story
- ☐ How They Handle the Good and Bad Times
- ☐ Can They Dust Themselves Off if Told No
- ☐ Complicated or Simple Business Model (should be simple)
- ☐ Profit Model
- ☐ Revenue Model
- ☐ Costs vs. Profit
- ☐ Industry Lens
- ☐ Financials
- ☐ Marketing and Sales
- ☐ New Funds

You may feel I'm overstating due diligence, but neglecting it can lead to significant financial losses.

In 2008, the world witnessed the unveiling of the largest Ponzi scheme in history, orchestrated by Bernie Madoff, which defrauded investors of billions of dollars. Many of the victims had blindly trusted the businessman and did not conduct proper due diligence, leading to significant losses.[31]

In 2015, it came to light how important it is to understand an industry you invest in and ask the right questions as part of your due diligence. An emission scandal caused a significant drop in a company's share prices

---

31   Hayes, A. 2023. *Bernie Madoff: Who He Was, How His Ponzi Scheme Worked.* Retrieved from https://www.investopedia.com/terms/b/bernard-madoff.asp.

because they concealed using illegal software to cheat tests. This resulted in numerous lawsuits and investors losing billions of dollars, too.[32]

In 2016, when a company's claims of their technology were fully investigated, it was found to be not as advertised and ineffective. Worse, there were concerns since the early 2000s about it, and the company collapsed, costing investors billions.[33]

Analyzing the risks of a fractional ownership investment is very important.

There are benefits when choosing the best investment for you.

Remember, alternative investing includes crowdfunding, peer-to-peer lending, and **Fractional Ownership**. With fractional ownership, you can buy a share of an asset. This allows you to invest in high-value assets that may have been out of reach otherwise and share in the returns and risks with other investors.

Now, let's talk about choosing a fractional ownership investment based on your investment goals and risk tolerance. It's essential to do your due diligence and research, but avoid common mistakes such as investing in assets you don't understand or failing to diversify your portfolio. Remember, fractional ownership is just one part of a well-diversified portfolio, so consider other types of investments as well.

---

32   Hotten, R. 2015. *Volkswagen: The scandal explained.* Retrieved from https://www.bbc.com/news/business-34324772.

33   Pflanzer, LR. 2019. The rise and fall of Theranos, the blood-testing startup that went from Silicon Valley darling to facing fraud charges. Retrieved from https://www.businessinsider.com/the-history-of-silicon-valley-unicorn-theranos-and-ceo-elizabeth-holmes-2018-5#but-holmes-was-not-deterred-holmes-went-on-to-drop-out-of-stanford-university-in-2003-at-the-age-of-19-to-start-theranos-which-was-then-called-real-time-cures-she-was-inspired-both-by-her-grandfathers-medical-career-and-her-summer-2003-internship-at-the-genome-institute-of-singapore-2.

But what's next?

How can you continue to grow and thrive in alternative investing and fractional ownership? The answer lies in innovation and growth.

As the market for alternative investments continues to grow, it's important to stay on the cutting edge of new strategies and techniques. By continually seeking out fresh concepts, techniques, and helpful resources, you can position yourself for success.

Stay ahead of the curve by joining like-minded investment groups and organizations, attending conferences and seminars, and reading industry articles. By staying up-to-date on the latest developments and trends, you can be sure you're always making informed decisions and maximizing your returns.

So, whether you're just starting out in the world of alternative investing or a seasoned pro, remember that the key to success is to stay innovative, hungry, and never stop learning. With the right mindset and the right tools at your disposal, you can achieve your financial dreams and secure your future through the power of fractional ownership and alternative investing.

Again, take inspiration from Kevin.

Kevin's success can be attributed to his willingness to learn and adopt a growth mindset. To reinvent. He acknowledges that he did not know much when he started, and his education came from mentoring programs and partnering with experienced investors like RAD Diversified. He learned from his failures, persevered, and continues to challenge what the stereotypical ideals of financial success mean.

As you explore the world of fractional ownership, you will realize that gone are the days when traditional investment methods were the only way to secure your financial future. You have the basics now and many options before you. Stay caught up, take control of your financial future, and join this financial movement.

Chapter Review

If you'd like to practice what you've learned in this chapter, I invite you to check out the exercises at this link: https://therad.com/moneyshackles/workbook

The chapter exercises encourage you to list different types of fractional ownership investments and their benefits, acknowledge the common mistakes to avoid when choosing from this list, and decide which ones will help you achieve your financial goals.

1. If you're stuck in traditional investing routes, you may believe insufficient funds, time, energy, or knowledge are the *Obstacles Preventing Investing*. However, alternative investing options like fractional ownership can provide access to high-value assets and potentially higher returns, allowing you to diversify your portfolio and achieve financial freedom.

2. Breaking free from traditional investing and exploring alternative investments like fractional ownership can help you achieve the Redefined American Dream. Still, conducting thorough due diligence is crucial to understand the potential risks and returns. Use the RADD Keys and *Business Checklist* before investing.

3. When choosing an investment with *Fractional Ownership Benefits*, it's important to consider your investment goals and risk tolerance and avoid common mistakes such as investing in assets you don't understand or failing to diversify your portfolio. To stay ahead of the curve in alternative investing, join like-minded investment groups and organizations,

attend conferences and seminars, and read industry articles to continually seek fresh concepts and techniques.

Can owning alternative investments be the right step toward your dreams? Owning alternative investments, like fractional ownership, can be a viable option for achieving your financial goals and diversifying your portfolio. However, it's crucial to reflect on your goals, stay up-to-date on the latest investment news and trends, and do your due diligence by evaluating potential investment opportunities considering factors such as the founder's story, the business model for profitability, existing revenue, and obstacles to success.

CHAPTER 7

DIVERSIFY YOUR INVESTMENTS FOR LONG-TERM SUCCESS

What are the advantages of diversification for your portfolio?

You've worked hard to earn your money, and the last thing you want is to lose it all in one fell swoop. That's why diversification is important. By spreading your investments across multiple assets, you can help protect yourself from losses and mitigate risk.

Imagine you've invested all your savings into one company, and that company suddenly goes bankrupt. You'd lose everything. Yet, if you had invested in multiple companies or assets, the impact of that one bankruptcy would be much smaller. "Don't put all of your eggs in one basket," really starts to make sense.

This is the power of diversification.

There are many strategies you can use to diversify your portfolio. These strategies include diversifying across different asset classes.

- Real Estate provides a hedge against inflation, passive

income generation, and potential value appreciation, encompassing REITs, farms, vacation rentals, houses, apartments, self-storage, and more.

- Commodities can diversify portfolios, act as an inflation hedge, and serve as a safe haven during market downturns, covering precious gems and metals, oil and gas partnerships, farming, and timber.

- Art and Collectibles offer high returns, protection against inflation, and personal satisfaction to collectors, including vintage cars, rare books, and historical/entertainment memorabilia.

- Private Equity presents high-return potential and allows investors to participate in private companies' growth and success, spanning angel investing, growth equity, and leveraged buyouts (LBOs).

- Peer-to-Peer Lending provides higher yields than traditional fixed-income investments, portfolio diversification, and credit access for non-qualifying borrowers, such as medical/equipment financing, small business loans, and social impact bonds.

- Infrastructure offers stable, long-term cash flows, often supported by government contracts/regulations and inflation-protected returns, encompassing renewable energy projects, transportation, and data centers.

- Intellectual Property: Can offer high returns on investment and provides legal protection for the owner's intellectual property rights. This includes: Patents, Software, or Media and Video Game Rights.

Of course, before jumping into any investment, do your due diligence.

Diversification can empower you to take control.

Ultimately, the **Power of Diversification** is about building a portfolio that can weather the ups and downs of the market and provide you with a solid foundation for a secure and prosperous future. To reiterate, it is best to utilize alternative investments to get your money working for you and embrace the Law of Abundance. You should be making a plan you can follow through with.

Jeff and Robin Thomas, who are great folks, learned this.

They sought stable returns that traditional investments couldn't provide. As you know, Robin had a difficult divorce and had no retirement plan despite owning successful businesses. She was starting from zero in her fifties.

Robin says, "While I had a little bit of money saved here and there, it wasn't enough to ensure my financial future. For me, this meant reinventing myself as a single woman in my fifties. I was dating Jeff at the time and I had nothing to fall back on. Despite owning two successful businesses, I realized that I needed a plan for my retirement. Social Security isn't a guarantee, and it may not be enough to support my lifestyle when I retire."

"So, I had to start from scratch and learn how to build my wealth through alternative investments," Robin adds. "While I made a good amount of money through my businesses, I needed a strategy to secure my financial future."

In fact, within 36 months, Robin broke seven figures through alternative investments. A testament to the potential of investing in non-traditional ways.

Jeff's story is similar, "My background was really in sales, and with the downturn in the economy in 2008-2009, it forced me to find another avenue to make some money." He knew what he had to do, he had to do something different. "Maybe it's time to move into other directions."

As a professional, Jeff had always been fascinated by real estate.

He even obtained a license but never quite pursued it with as much passion as he had hoped. However, a recent revelation had stirred his desire to make a change. From financial books and a few classes, he realized he needed to take some tangible steps to make his dreams of success a reality. Driven by a newfound sense of motivation, Jeff followed many of the steps of making money work for him, choosing the right investments, and diversifying his portfolio, and he has seen his wealth grow.

"At that point... I think the biggest difference for me was actually moving forward on something," Jeff says. "That has changed my life greatly over the last 10 years that I've been doing this (investing) now."

Like Jeff and Robin, you also can expand your diversification techniques with alternative investments. There's an art, a science, risks, and regulations, but ultimately the choices are yours.

To get started, here's a list of platforms for alternative investments:

- AngelList (https://wellfound.com/): This platform connects early-stage founders with investors and startup resources and provides investors with access to alternative investment opportunities in venture capital, private equity, and real estate.

- Crowdfund Insider (https://www.crowdfundinsider.com/): This website provides news, analysis, and data about the alternative finance industry, including crowdfunding and peer-to-peer lending platforms.

- DealMaker (https://www.dealmaker.tech/): The leading technology provider in self-hosted raises, no matter what type of raise, DealMaker can provide founders with the support to raise digitally and manage the lifecycle afterward.

- LendingClub (https://www.lendingclub.com/):

LendingClub is a peer-to-peer lending platform that connects borrowers with investors. Investors can invest in various loans, including personal, small business, and auto refinancing loans.

- Masterworks (https://www.masterworks.com/): Masterworks is a platform that allows investors to invest in shares of fine art. The platform acquires and manages a collection of high-end art pieces and allows investors to purchase shares of the collection. Investors can benefit from the potential appreciation of the value of the art over time.

- Republic (https://republic.com/): Republic is a platform that offers equity crowdfunding investments in startups and real estate projects. The platform aims to democratize access to early-stage investments globally by allowing individual investors to invest alongside venture capitalists and angel investors.

- StartEngine (https://www.startengine.com/): An equity crowdfunding investment platform of various types, one of the largest portals in the US, also offers secondary trading.

- Wefunder (https://wefunder.com/): One of the leading equity crowdfunding portals in the US, offering investors many different categories of early-stage investing.

- Yieldstreet (https://www.yieldstreet.com/): This platform provides access to alternative investment opportunities in real estate, art finance, commercial lending, and more.

When making decisions in life, there's always a choice between being selfish or taking the abundance approach. In the world of alternative investments, you can focus only on your wealth or the growth and expansion of your network.

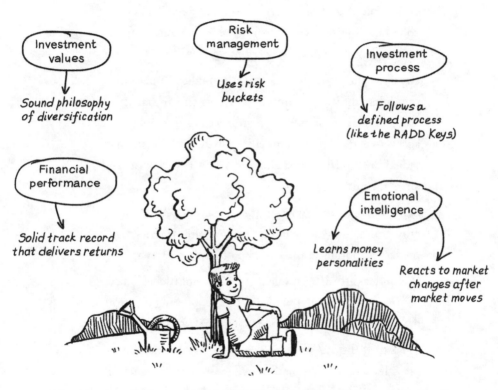

A good investor can live sustainably with both their active income and investments

Diversification is not only about spreading your investments across different assets but can also be a way of making smart decisions.

If you're not actively growing your money or making it work for you, you may feel the pain of missed opportunities and stagnation. It's easy to get caught up in the daily grind and forget that your money should work just as hard as you are. You must take action to grow and invest your money to reach financial goals and feel the stress of financial uncertainty. Yet, there is always time to start making your money work for you and taking control of your financial future.

This is where your Financial Decision Tree will grow as you become a **Good Investor.**

Good investors find decent investment opportunities and make a return on their investment. They mitigate risks as the market moves because they know their relationship with money and their investment values and can diversify assets, and have a defined evaluation process that balances and sustains their track record.

Follow the same process with the starting point of the Financial Decision Tree, list a set of criteria, then evaluate by scoring each one. The scores can be based on a scale of 0 to 10, with 10 being the best possible score.

To be a good investor, you need to know how to identify decent investment opportunities, but it doesn't require you to have extraordinary financial expertise or resources. It requires a willingness to learn, a long-term perspective, and a commitment to disciplined and patient investing practices. You don't have to be a millionaire to be a successful investor. Many successful individuals, from entrepreneurs to corporate executives, have achieved financial success through good investing practices.

This will benefit you if you follow these decision-making strategies to break free of the "Money Shackles."

Remember, even seemingly safe and reliable investments can carry risks, and it's essential to diversify our portfolios and not rely solely on one stock or sector.

After discussing the benefits and risks of alternative investments, it's important to remember that traditional investments can also carry their own risks. The collapse of Lehman Brothers in 2008 was a stark reminder that even the most esteemed and solid blue-chip companies can fall prey to unexpected financial turmoil and result in catastrophic consequences.[34]

Blue-chip refers to a well-established, financially sound company with a long track record of consistent performance. Financial advisors often recommend it to their clients as a relatively low-risk investment with the potential for steady returns over time.

It makes sense, right?

If you didn't "put your eggs in different baskets," you might have felt major repercussions over a decade ago.

The story of Lehman Brothers is a cautionary tale about what can happen when diversification is not managed properly. The hundred-year-old investment bank, known for its success on Wall Street, became greedy and focused solely on making money for itself. Bankers neglected their responsibilities and failed to manage their investments effectively, leading to the bank's collapse. This included:

- The investment bank did not adequately diversify its investments, focusing on the mortgage-backed securities market.

- The investment bank's over-reliance on the mortgage-backed securities market caused significant exposure to the subprime market, resulting in the collapse when it experienced a downturn.

---

34   Kenton, W. 2022. *Lehman Brothers: History, Collapse, Role in the Great Recession.* Retrieved from https://www.investopedia.com/terms/l/lehman-brothers.asp.

- The investment bank had a large amount of debt relative to its equity, leaving it vulnerable to market fluctuations.

- The investment bank had poor risk management practices, failing to anticipate the severity of the market downturn.

- The investment bank lacked transparency, making it difficult to understand financial statements and not being forthcoming about its exposure to the subprime mortgage market.

These failures caused a financial event that sent shockwaves throughout the global financial system and triggered the Great Recession of 2008.

I advocate expanding investments in alternative investment fields. Making many smaller micro-investments in different risk buckets can reduce overall exposure to portfolios. Unlike traditional investments, one does not need to invest much capital into one venture to achieve success. Instead, smaller amounts can be invested into several ventures, increasing the chances of profitable returns.

Think about it.

Investing $1,000 into thirty companies may yield significant returns, as it only requires one or two successful investments to make a significant financial impact. When considering diversification and alternative investments, understanding the differences between various levels of companies is important.

Observing companies that achieve success through the highest level of management is important.

The great American Dream success stories often originated from unique founders' tales of passion, creativity, intensity, and perseverance. These individuals pursued a vision of greatness by striving to become the best in their field or completely revolutionize an industry. They actively looked for gaps or missing links in their industry, believing they could be more effective by operating the best system.

When considering investment companies, it's important to know the difference between a "Babysitter" and a "True Operator."

"Babysitters" are more common than people realize and don't serve a valuable function. They babysit your money, may have a few good quarters, but eventually the investment companies will lose your money. These companies may excel at attracting investors and telling a compelling story, or perhaps they were able to secure significant capital, but they don't really know what they're doing. At the end of the day, "Babysitters" are not adaptable to market changes and typically yield lower returns.

"True Operators" are the opposite of "Babysitters" and can significantly impact investment returns. Founders like Jeff Bezos, Steve Jobs, and Warren Buffett come to mind because of their direct involvement in the DNA of their businesses. However, I often find myself repeatedly speaking with real estate funds that don't engage in real estate themselves. From the start of our conversation, it becomes clear that their real estate knowledge comes from a book or preconceived notions of something they heard, and they haven't put in the effort to truly understand the industry. "True Operators," on the other hand, have an in-depth understanding of every aspect of their business and industry. They consistently generate higher returns and are a more reliable alternative investment.

If you have doubts about an investment opportunity or notice any irregularities in a company's financial statements or management practices, it's essential to conduct further investigation before investing. In my experience, investing in companies with a proven track record and sound financial management practices is crucial to achieving long-term success in investing. By taking the time to thoroughly research potential investments and ensure they meet your standards for transparency and accountability, you can help mitigate risk and maximize your chances of achieving your investment goals.

My experience in the real estate industry has taught me that success depends on understanding the value of a location and aligning it with an investment strategy. By using a combination of art and science, I have been able to make informed decisions that have led to my financial success.

Zillow was an example of a "Babysitter" that excelled at technology in 2021 but wasn't a "True Operator." Zillow lost hundreds of millions of dollars because it used flawed decision-making processes and relied too much on data science.[35] They were missing what I call the "Art of Investing," which involves reading market changes, understanding location-specific rules, being aware of cultural influences, and having extensive knowledge of American history.

What about the art and science of finding great investments?

To break out of the "Money Shackles" and achieve financial freedom, you must master the art and science of finding great financial investments. The **Art and Science of Investing** involve a combination of analytical skills, financial knowledge, and strategic decision-making. Art relies on the strategy created from quantitative and qualitative variables from a macroeconomic perspective and science relies on mathematical models and metrics.

But it's not just about crunching numbers and analyzing data. You must also use your creativity and intuition to identify unique investment opportunities that add value to your portfolio.

Let's be real here: investing always carries risks. You can't just rush into things and hope for the best. That's why diversification is key. By keeping your money growing through diversification, you can achieve financial security and freedom.

Now, I know diversifying investments may not sound like the most exciting thing in the world. I know, it's important. It can help you to maximize returns and minimize risks. If you're aiming to be a good investor, it will help towards generating enough capital to have money put away that

35   Lambert, L. 2022. *Zillow's $6 billion home flipping business was a disaster. Now, a cooling housing market could foil its comeback plan.* Retrieved from https://fortune.com/2022/06/02/zillow-6-billion-home-flipping-business-housing-market-fortune-500/.

you could live off of in addition to your income. This can provide numerous benefits and opportunities for long-term financial growth.

With determination and persistence, you can overcome any challenges and continue to grow your money through diversification. Don't let fear hold you back. Take the time to master the art and science of finding great investments, and you'll be on your way to your ideal success.

Chapter Review

If you'd like to practice what you've learned
in this chapter, I invite you to check out the
exercises at this link:
https://therad.com/moneyshackles/workbook

The chapter exercises encourage you to attend investment work-shops or webinars hosted by financial experts, create a mock investment portfolio to track and adjust over time while analyzing companies' financial statements, and write a detailed investment plan and review it regularly by staying up to date on market trends and news to inform investment decisions.

1.   ***The Power of Diversification*** can help protect against losses and mitigate risk by investing in multiple asset classes, including alternative investments such as real estate, commodities, and peer-to-peer lending. Use specialized platforms to start investing in these areas.

2.   A ***Good Investor***'s decisions require discipline, education, and diversification to avoid stagnation and minimize risks. The Lehman Brothers' story highlights the importance of managing diversification properly. Investing in alternative fields with smaller micro-investments can reduce exposure and increase profitability.

3.   Maximize your financial success by utilizing the skills within the ***Art and Science of Investing.*** It will help you identify "True Operators" through thorough research and investing in companies with sound financial management practices. Diversify your portfolio to

achieve long-term financial security and freedom.
Fear should not hold you back. Determination and
persistence can lead to success.

What are the advantages of diversification for your portfolio?
Diversifying your portfolio by investing in multiple asset classes,
including alternative investments, and using specialized platforms is
crucial to minimize risk and protect against losses. Smart investment
decisions require discipline, education, and diversification to achieve
long-term financial security and freedom. Identifying "True Operators"
with thorough research in companies with sound financial management
practices can maximize your financial success while not letting fear hold
you back.

CHAPTER 8

LEVERAGING REAL ESTATE

What are REITs, and how can they create wealth and financial security?

One of my first mentors told me, "When you make other people money, you will always make money."

It's more than just about money, though.

Making yourself useful, resourceful, impactful, and important will return capital to your life. This is how we run our model and business at RAD Diversified (RADD). Prioritizing the growth of others. I believe my talent in helping others grow is through real estate.

Real estate investing is a fantastic way to build wealth.

I know this, but when I was younger, boy, did I fight it.

I fought this belief repeatedly because my parents were both the best and the worst real estate investors ever. My childhood was constantly up-and-down due to my parents' addictions and financial struggles. During different cycles, they owned a racetrack, an apartment complex, an income-producing parking property next to state fairgrounds, and more. However, they also lost all these properties due to addiction, bad financial management, and lack of diversification. They broke many of the rules that I laid out for you in previous chapters.

I've worked as a successful real estate consultant and investor for over 15 years, and I can confidently say that I've "seen it all" in the real estate industry. When I was 25, I remember watching a financial wealth infomercial late at night on PBS. At that time, I had finally made some money and wondered what to do with it. So, I went on a knowledge journey determined not to be like my parents; my goal was to have something better and stronger. During this journey, I wrote down many things about what I wanted my life to be.

Looking back, it's frustrating to see how many people still taught outdated techniques from 10, 15, or even 20 years ago—especially in the constantly evolving real estate industry. I've seen others more focused on selling education, consulting, and mentoring services, using questionable techniques that don't align with my values. In addition, some real estate investors are more interested in maximizing profits at the property owner's expense. I knew there had to be a better way to approach real estate investing, and I was determined to find it.

In 2015, I was falling into a trap I had seen with so many education companies. I was selling real estate education, buying trips, and online resources. Students told us repeatedly that the hands-on approach was the most effective learning experience, but when I looked at their results, they were minimal and I hated it.

One night after a trip with 22 students and seeing not one buy a property, I asked everyone why. They said we taught them well and showed them good deals, but doing it alone was too much. They said, "Dutch, put your money where your mouth is and invest side by side hand in hand with us." It was one of those defining moments that changed everything. Twenty-one of those 22 students invested in properties with me, and three years later, the 22nd student, Ron Johnson, a retired Secret Service agent, also invested.

My team and I started our first real estate fund that year. We worked hard, feeling like we were ceaselessly grinding away like characters in the 2006 movie "The Pursuit of Happyness." We knew something was building, and we were destined for more. As time went by, we began to see encouraging returns. Then, in 2017, we realized the returns were real and solid. We also completed individual deals and made substantial profits. When I partnered with other investors, my returns increased significantly. Looking back, I realize that all my early real estate deals involved great partners.

Looking back, it's easy to forget the hard work and grind it took to get to this point. That's the reality of building something from scratch. It's not a sudden switch from one life to another. The journey is sometimes too long for those who need instant gratification. I realized there's a choice between taking a selfish approach or one based in abundance regarding real estate. I chose to focus on the abundant approach for the long-term well-being of those around me and prioritize the growth and success of our team, staff, and investors.

Real estate investing can be challenging for many people, with significant barriers to entry, limited opportunities for diversification, and the complexities of managing tenants, repairs, and contractors. We recognized the struggles faced by everyday Americans in breaking free from the "Money Shackles" and gaining access to real estate investing opportunities. While individual investments, stock markets, and private funds have historically been available primarily to accredited investors with significant wealth, we saw the potential for change with the passing of the JOBS Act. This landmark legislation has opened the door to new investment opportunities for all Americans, providing greater access to alternative investments and the potential for significant long-term returns.

The JOBS Act made investing in real estate a team game, particularly through Fractional Ownership models.

It gives investors a great way to build wealth and achieve financial stability without being alone and taking all the risks. The process involves purchasing, owning, and managing properties to generate income and appreciation over time. It creates the benefits of Real Investing while sharing in the risk. Like all investments, you must do your homework and learn how to choose the companies to partner with.

I always make sure to assess our competitive advantages carefully. I've noticed that some companies just throw money at real estate without knowing what they're doing, which I call "The Babysitter," which I first referred to in Chapter 7.

Companies should be "True Operators," meaning they strategically approach their investments and do their homework before moving. To succeed in real estate investing, using the right techniques for the right market conditions is important. This is something I've learned through a life of active real estate investing. The RADD way has helped people overcome financial obstacles and achieve their Redefined American Dreams.

The real estate market has long been regarded as a reliable and secure path to wealth and financial security.

I understand that barriers may prevent some individuals from accessing this valuable asset. That's why I'm dedicated to assisting people in entering the game and establishing their presence in the property market. We've developed a successful system at The RAD for collaborative investments that allow us to acquire income-generating residential and agricultural properties, offering an accessible path for those who want to make their mark in real estate.

It's important to keep an eye on your investment and stay informed, especially as an equity-based real estate investor. One of the benefits of investing in the real estate industry and other alternative investments is that they don't change daily, providing a certain amount of peace and stability to your portfolio.

When considering investing in alternative companies, evaluating their existing sales and transactions, determining their burn rate, and understanding the differences between high-risk and moderate-to-low-risk investments are important. By doing so, you can maximize your potential for financial success.

Starting in real estate, I had to figure out how to buy properties without money, including absorbing existing financing, doing subject-to-deals, and wholesaling. Yet, as our company grew, I moved on from that. Our general philosophy is that the more money we have working for us, the right way, the more returns we get. Having $10,000 won't make you much money, but getting to $100,000 or $1 million is where compounding makes a difference. It's a different level of looking at things.

Equity real estate investment trusts are not liquid investments.

They are about building equity, not trading money in and out like the stock market. We invest in assets that will grow and provide long-term returns, emphasizing stability and steady growth over short-term fluctuations.

Real Estate Investment Trusts (REITs) offer a way for people to invest in real estate without directly taking on all the risks and complexities of owning property. Here's why REITs are worth considering:

- Expert Management: REITs are typically run by real estate professionals, so you're likely to make more informed investment decisions and experience less risk.

- Passive Income: REITs generate income through rent and property appreciation, so you can get steady cash.

- Lower Investment Threshold: With REITs, you can invest in large-scale, institutional-quality real estate with a smaller upfront investment than you'd need for direct real estate investments.

Overall, REITs offer a way for people to get a piece of the real estate pie while avoiding some of the risks and headaches that come with own-ing property directly.

Our research team constantly monitors real estate and the U.S. market, considering past and future trends. For example, in 2021, we predicted the rise of interest rates and its impact on hyperinflation, which we had previously discussed in 2020 as a likely outcome of infus-ing lots of money into the economy. It's generally a good investment strategy to try and regularly make market predictions and analyze mar-ket trends, in order to move before the market moves. In 2022, I told my investors my beliefs that it was time to exit the crypto market as I saw potential challenges and problems ahead. Some investors were grateful for this advice, while others regretted not following it.

We adjust our investments accordingly based on these insights. For example, we invested in farmland as we anticipated supply chain issues and increased commodity prices due to the pandemic. By stay-ing informed and proactive in our investment strategy, we aim to make informed decisions. You'll have a sure sense of being in control of your money and your financial future.

It's essential to stay informed about market trends and potential changes in the real estate industry. Our research team monitors real estate and the U.S. market, considering past and future trends, and aims to provide investors with the tools and insights they need to make informed investment decisions.

Real estate investing offers many benefits, including the potential for passive income and long-term appreciation. By owning rental proper-ties, you can generate regular income without working a traditional job, and the value of your properties can increase over time, allowing you to build long-term wealth.

With that in mind, let's look at some of the benefits of real estate investing. By leveraging the insights of our research team and staying informed, you'll have a sure sense of being in control of your money and your financial future. Taking a proactive approach and staying ahead of the curve is essential as we move forward in our journey of alternative investing. With this approach, you can maximize the potential benefits of real estate investing and achieve long-term financial security.

Keys to Real Estate Success

1. Gaining knowledge for understanding your investments.

2. Finding the right partners.

3. Minimizing risk through diversification.

4. Taking advantage of smaller investments through fractionalized ownership.

5. Investing with experienced "True Operators."

6. Investing for long-term success.

7. Protecting your investments with insurance and legal.

8. Choosing the right location.

9. Using value add techniques to increase returns.

10. Having a clear strategy with rules.

To succeed in real estate investing, it's important to have a clear strategy.

When choosing investment properties, it is important to conduct detailed research. In my companies, we describe our strategy as part of the **Diamond 5** principles.

1. Economic Philosophy: Thrive During Economic Recessions

2. Profit Strategy: Compound Acceleration

3. Acquisitions: Location, Location, Location (RADD Zone)

4. Diversify: Alternative Investments

5. Social Impact: Food and Water Security (Farmland), and Other Options

Before you start to worry, I'm going to walk you through the very strategy that uses the Diamond 5 in every aspect. With the right strategy and access to the right tools and resources, anyone can succeed in real estate investing, which is a time-tested path to long-term wealth.

ECONOMIC PHILOSOPHY

The real estate market changes during a recession.

Using alternative techniques like tax auctions, mortgage fore-closures, bank-owned properties, and HOA foreclosures to buy rental properties is important. These are actionable steps that reflect an underlying philosophy: know your timing. Knowing when to buy a property, like during times of hardship, to increase its equity and value during times of prosperity is smart.

When the time is right, buying at a "deep discount" and choosing an effective location are the next key principles.

PROFIT STRATEGY

As I previously mentioned in Chapter 1, compounding money puts it to work for you. When acquiring real estate, you can still utilize this stratagem as one of your techniques, but in a more nuanced way.

To wrap your head around this concept of a property being "discounted," you should aim to maximize your returns by selecting properties likely to appreciate over time. This means paying close attention to local real estate trends and assessing factors such as location, surroundings, and potential for renovations. You can start building a successful real estate portfolio by doing your homework and making informed decisions.

When making investment decisions, it is crucial to know the difference between a property that is likely to appreciate 1%, 5%, 10%, or even more in the next 12 months. Booming economies provide fewer properties at under-market prices. The strategy of Value becomes very important. Recession provides a better chance for off-market properties and buying a discount is critical.

When buying real estate, be aware that agents may try to persuade you to increase your offer. You should not counter your own offer because it gives the other party an advantage. If the agent is unwilling to make a counteroffer at first, wait. Compromising your offer will only reduce your profit margin.

It is important to buy at the right value, whether under-market, off-market, retail, or at foreclosure auctions. The technique for this evolves with changes in the economy. In real estate, you can add value by choosing properties with the potential for growth. The goal is to increase the property's value by adding "income centers," "profit centers," or square footage.

Value-added real estate helps you turn an underperforming property into a valuable asset. It involves you doing careful analysis and planning strategically to find a property with growth potential, then coming up with a solid plan to add value. This could include adding "income centers" to your property by renting out unused spaces, adding amenities that increase rental income. You can also find "profit centers" by reducing operating costs (thereby increasing profitability). With the right approach, you can transform underperforming properties into valuable assets that generate consistent cash flow and build wealth over time.

Adding square footage is one surefire way to add value to a real estate investment. You can get more usable space from a property by renovating, adding to the structure, or rearranging the layout. Once you've got more space to offer, you can attract new tenants and bump up your potential rental income.

These value variables are why you can approach real estate investment with a logic-based formula that considers factors such as location, economic trends, and market demand. Investors who use a data-driven approach to analyze these variables can make informed decisions about where to invest and potentially see higher returns.

Using a logic-based formula can help eliminate emotional decision-making and increase the chances of success in the real estate market. Remember: while formulas can guide decision-making, they shouldn't be the sole factor in the decision-making process.

In an inflationary real estate market, value-add investing is important to understand. This approach to investing involves improving neglected properties or adding square footage with the primary goal of increasing the value of an asset.

An often-overlooked part of this formula that is essential to understand is how property values may be projected to change over time. Finding profitable changes can greatly affect your potential returns. One useful technique involves overlaying a city map with a valuation map. This can help investors determine the direction of property value changes in a specific area.

As you expand your earnings, accelerate the accumulation of your wealth by cycling the money through more properties.

ACQUISITIONS

Another factor is **the RADD Zone**, or the sweet spot where we like to buy property in the best location.

Choosing an effective location is a key factor to consider between different properties. Downtown areas and landmarks such as hospitals, universities, and stadiums are valuable and can significantly impact a property's value. Core landmarks, in particular, have two sides to consider. On one side, a highly appreciating market may be called the valley. Conversely, a slower, more stagnant market may be called the desert.

The RADD Zone often occurs at the overlap of two valleys and has easy access to nearby amenities and transportation. For example, the intersection of a college and a gentrified area combines the high growth potential of the two landmarks. These locations tend to perform best over the long term.

Using a smart value-add strategy with the perfect location, you can set yourself up for a successful investment that yields impressive returns and builds wealth for years.

DIVERSIFY

Let's look at two popular alternative investment options in real estate that will help to diversify your portfolio: owning rental properties and fractionalized ownership.

Rental properties are a type of real estate investment where you purchase a property, such as a house or an apartment building, with the intention of renting it out to tenants. It can be a great way to generate passive income, as the rent collected from tenants can help cover the mortgage and other expenses while providing a steady income stream. You also can get the benefits of compounding appreciation and the tax benefits of depreciation.

However, investing in rental properties also requires significant capital and time. You will need to have enough money to cover the down payment, closing costs, and ongoing expenses such as maintenance and repairs. You will also need the time and resources to find and manage tenants, collect rent, and handle any issues that may arise.

Another option for real estate investment is fractionalized ownership. REITs are one type of fractionalized ownership. Companies that own and manage a portfolio of income-producing properties, such as rentals, shopping centers, apartment complexes, and farms. As an investor in a REIT, you can purchase shares of the company and receive a portion of the income generated from the properties.

Thanks to the JOBS Act, non-traded public REITs have emerged as a compelling alternative. These REITs offer all the advantages of traded REITs but without the volatility of daily market fluctuations. *They have audited financials, third-party evaluations, and Securities Exchange Commission (SEC) qualifications and are accessible to everyone.*

One of the benefits of investing in REITs is that it allows you to diversify your real estate portfolio without the need for a significant amount of capital or time commitment. Public REITs are regulated by the SEC and it provides additional transparency and oversight.

However, like any investment, there are risks involved with REITs. Market fluctuations and changes in interest rates can impact the value of your investment, and not all REITs perform equally. It is important to research and evaluate the potential risks and rewards. Finding "True Operators" can make a significant difference.

Both rental properties and fractionalized alternatives offer unique opportunities for real estate investment. Whether you invest in rental properties or REITs (or both), it is important to understand the potential risks and rewards and make informed decisions based on your financial goals and resources.

SOCIAL IMPACT

One of my real estate investment strategies is centered around security needs.

This strategy recognizes food and water security as necessary, particularly through American-owned farmland and ranches. Alternatively, other strategies could include housing security and supporting local economies with Qualified Opportunity Zone funds, or building up infrastructure security through transportation, sewage systems, and energy.

The role of agriculture in sustaining communities is critical because of its support of the production of food and the preservation of water resources. The acquisition of farmland allows for the investment in sustainable agricultural practices, such as organic farming or regenerative agriculture. By investing in farmland, investors can contribute to ensuring a stable food supply, promoting sustainable farming methods, and protecting valuable water sources.

Additionally, this social impact strategy may encompass exploring other options, such as investing in affordable housing projects or renewable energy initiatives. Aligning real estate

investments with social impact goals, investors have the opportunity to make a positive difference in communities and the
environment while achieving long-term financial success.

You need to consider several critical factors for success-ful real estate investing.

As an aspiring real estate investor, you must know how to evaluate
potential investments and which factors to consider while building your
portfolio. Additionally, avoiding common mistakes that could jeopar-
dize the success of your investment is crucial. With the right knowledge
and strategy, you can make informed decisions and set yourself up for
success in the world of real estate investing.

Common Real Estate Mistakes

1. Following the herd and buying retail.

2. Buying because there's a new development.

3. Avoid the unicorn.[36]

4. Giving your money to someone with no experience.

5. Investing just because someone you know is.

6. Trusting the due diligence of others.

7. Buying for the short-term.

8. Buying virtually without a plan.

---

36 A unicorn refers to a real estate deal or property that offers an extraordinary return on
investment or comes with exceptionally favorable terms. This might be a property purchased
at a significantly undervalued price, in a high-demand location, with potential for significant
appreciation or rental income.

9.   Buying the cheapest real estate.

10.   Using unlicensed or cheap contractors.

Finally, it's important to avoid common mistakes that can be detrimental to your real estate investment success. These include overpaying for a property, underestimating the cost of repairs or renovations, and failing to conduct proper due diligence on the property and the surrounding market. Additionally, it's important to have a solid understanding of your financing options and to carefully manage your cash flow to ensure you can cover unexpected expenses.

The end goal of investing is to achieve financial freedom and lead the lifestyle we desire, a goal that I share with countless other investors. Having achieved financial freedom, I remain committed to aiding others to reach the same goal.

Through the creation of a tight-knit Tribe of investors and employees, our company has grown to become a large family, with even the children of our employees and investors interning with us to learn more about the business. Many have become valuable contributors to our team.

As an investor, one of the things I enjoy most about my job is being able to open doors for the next generation. Understanding and knowledge are key to success, and I am passionate about sharing that knowledge with others.

With the right knowledge and strategy, we can grow our money faster, which has a significant long-term impact.

Real estate can be a powerful tool for achieving your financial goals and your American Dream. Whether that means generating a passive income to support your lifestyle, building long-term wealth, or creating a legacy for future generations, real estate investing can help you get there. As with any investment, it's important to approach real estate investing with a clear strategy and a commitment to staying informed and engaged with the market.

Chapter Review

If you'd like to practice what you've learned in this chapter, I invite you to check out the exercises at this link: https://therad.com/moneyshackles/workbook

The chapter exercises encourage you to analyze REITs and their potential for creating wealth and financial security, list the risks and benefits associated with various types of properties for real estate investing and identify the factors that affect the success of real estate investments, including passive income, appreciation, and taxes.

1. Real estate investing can be a powerful tool for building wealth and helping others grow. You may have reservations due to past experiences, but the truth is that it offers many benefits, including passive income and long-term appreciation. If you understand the *Keys to Real Estate Success*, then you will understand the real estate funds that can wisely invest successfully.

2. REITs are a great way to invest in real estate without directly owning property. They offer a way to invest in real estate while emphasizing stability and steady growth over short-term fluctuations. Equity real estate investment trusts may not be liquid investments, but they are about building equity, which can lead to long-term wealth.

   • To succeed in real estate investing, it's essential to have a clear strategy like *RADD's Diamond 5* principles. You will see potential long-term growth if you or the REIT you are interested in investing in can clarify what is their economic philosophy, profit strategy, acquisitions metrics, diversification portfolio, and data-driven social impact interests.

3. You need to have a clear strategy and conduct detailed research to succeed in real estate. Maximizing your returns by selecting properties that are likely to appreciate over time, and avoiding *Common Real Estate Mistakes*, will ensure your real estate investing can be a powerful tool for achieving your financial goals and creating a legacy.

What are REITs, and how can they create wealth and financial security? REITs are an investment vehicle that encourages fractional ownership, emphasizes stability and steady growth over short-term fluctuations, and can be a great way to build long-term wealth through building equity. By conducting detailed research and selecting the right investments, including REITs, real estate investing has the potential to help you reach your dreams.

CHAPTER 9

NOT UNDERSTANDING YOUR TAXES COULD COST YOU YOUR BUSINESS

What are the tips for choosing the right team? Why do taxes matter in achieving your Redefined American Dream?

When I began making money, one of the first things I understood was that I was paying a lot of taxes.

Although it never occurred to me whether or not I should pay taxes, my focus was on earning more money with my investments. To this end, I used one main principle you probably heard me say: begin your journey toward gaining knowledge. *Please note: I am not an expert in taxation, you should always seek the help of a professional in this area.*

These are some of the essential realizations that have helped me. I believe:

1. All Americans should have a business.

2. All Americans should own real estate.

3. Your tax professional should be familiar with business and real estate.

4. Real estate is one of the great vehicles for utilizing the tax code in America.

5. Don't go with a professional who just says let me do your taxes, and you won't have to pay them.

My journey with taxation began on a rocky path, as I lacked even the most basic tax knowledge. I didn't understand concepts like credit scores or the role of a tax professional. In hindsight, it may seem simple, but I had no idea in my twenties and without proper training. It wasn't until I finally found a tax professional that I learned to limit my tax exposure without breaking the rules.

Unfortunately, due to my previous lack of knowledge, the following audit resulted in my owing hundreds of thousands of dollars to the IRS. It was a costly lesson, but it laid a foundation for understanding the importance of compliance and regulation as a public company.

When working towards achieving your Redefined American Dream through investments, it's essential to understand the regulations and tax codes that may affect your investments.

These rules can significantly impact your investment portfolio, which, in turn, can affect your returns and financial goals. By staying informed and aware of these **Tax Codes and Regulations**, you can make informed investment decisions to help you succeed in your investment journey.

One type of tax that can impact your investments is capital gains tax. This tax is applied to the profits you make from selling an investment. The tax on capital gains depends on how long you've held the investment. Short-term capital gains (investments held for less than a year) are taxed more than long-term capital gains (investments held for more than a year). Therefore, it's often a good strategy to hold onto investments for longer periods to take advantage of lower tax rates.

Another type of tax to consider is the dividend tax. This tax is applied to the income you receive from dividends paid by stocks you own. The dividend tax rate can vary depending on your income level and how long you've held the stock. One strategy to minimize dividend taxes is to invest in stocks that don't pay dividends but instead reinvest their profits into the company. This can help you avoid paying taxes on the income until you sell the stock.

Understanding regulations and tax codes can prevent unnecessary penalties and fees. Certain investments may be subject to specific regulations or tax codes, so it is important to adhere to these rules to avoid costly penalties. You must also understand how regulations and tax codes can impact the potential returns on your investments. Doing so lets you make informed decisions that help you maximize your returns and achieve your financial goals.

It's also important to note that regulations and tax codes are constantly evolving, so staying up-to-date on these changes is crucial for successful investing. Developing a customized strategy for navigating regulations and tax codes can help you avoid any changes that may impact your investments.

Financial education should be easy.

You should be utilizing a few math principles to make money and exchange it as a financial rule. But how many are taught any financial principles before leaving high school at 18 years old, especially how to maximize income and appreciate diverse sources of capital for financial freedom?

Between the Freedom Chart, Financial Decision Tree, and the **Tax Circle**, you will now have the education to make your money work for you.

To make money work for you, it means it has to move.

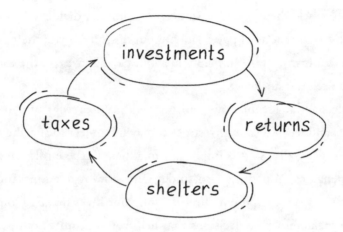

When first starting out, your **investments** should be a percentage of your income. If you're utilizing borrowing to compound your returns, then that percentage should be included in your calculations.

Your **returns** from your investments should be cycled through the other investments to increase returns. As these are part of your capital gains, you will want to protect them.

To protect your investments and returns, you'll want to leverage your money and cycle it through **shelters**. *Yes, I said shelter*—and tax shelters are not like the movies or offshore accounts. A tax shelter is a legal way to reduce taxes by utilizing deductions, credits, and exemptions, but is subject to strict regulations and scrutiny from tax authorities.[37]

These shelters will help depreciate your capital gains taxes. By utilizing business structures like LLCs or sole proprietorships to funnel your income, then hiring your kids and providing them a salary to appreciate their future retirements, and adding trusts and foundations to funnel your family's inheritance and legacy, you will be able to utilize additional different asset classes like 1031 Exchanges, Opportunity Zones, and retirement plans to diversify your investments.

As long as you appreciate the number of investment vehicles you have, you can maximize or speed up the process to your financial goals. Therefore, utilizing the shelters to their maximum potential will help depreciate the capital gains requirements within taxes and regulations.

To truly be financially free, you must maximize the benefits of the **tax** codes to the best situation.

You can decrease your taxes. You must educate yourself, utilize the shelters' regulations in support, then cycle the extra money into your investments to create greater returns and move through the Tax Circle again.

This is how you can make your money work for you, and keep it moving. The longer you can keep your money and the more money that works for you the faster you'll break the "Money Shackles".

Having the right team members assist you with various parts of your wealth journey is critical.

Tax strategists and legal counsel who understand your unique financial goals are critical to building a successful investment strategy and pursuing your Redefined American Dream.

---

37   Kagan, J. 2023. *Tax Shelter: Definitions, Examples, and Legal Issues.* Retrieved from https://www.investopedia.com/terms/t/taxshelter.asp.

I like to work with professionals with the heart of a teacher who does not simply instruct you on what to do and expects you to follow blindly. Rather, they instruct and answer questions that come up along the way, especially when you're considering your personalized *tax strategy*.

Not having a solid financial strategy was my downfall. It led to me paying an exorbitant amount in taxes, leaving me with less money to invest and grow my wealth. On top of that, I made the mistake of trusting the wrong professional to handle my finances, which resulted in me owing a substantial amount of money after an audit. These setbacks taught me a valuable lesson: having a clear financial strategy and working with the right professionals is absolutely crucial to avoiding unnecessary expenses and maximizing my financial success. From that point forward, I made it my mission to take control of my finances, educate myself on tax strategies, and surround myself with knowledgeable experts who have my best interests at heart. With a strategic approach and the right team in place, I am now able to minimize my tax liabilities and ensure that my hard-earned money is working for me, rather than being wasted on unnecessary payments.

Your tax strategy should be maximizing investment returns outside traditional markets (stocks, bonds, mutual funds, Exchange Traded Funds). It's crucial to have a diverse team of experts, including tax strategists and legal counsel, to develop tax-efficient investment strategies and ensure proper asset protection. It's also important to establish a solid foundation with liquid funds and various insurance types before investing in tangible assets. Considering each investment's purpose and timeline and selecting those that align with your financial goals can help create a powerful combination for long-term results.

There are tax strategies that can be used to amplify returns.

These strategies can involve the deferral of capital gains taxes and, in some cases, the elimination of taxes after certain criteria are met. Additionally, for business owners, other retirement planning strategies can be implemented, allowing reduced taxes owed while providing investment accounts further to put capital to work in a tax-advantaged way. Your **Tax Strategy** should include:

1031 Exchanges: When a business or piece of real estate is sold, and you have a gain, you generally have to pay taxes owed at the time of sale. Regarding investment real estate, IRC section 1031 spells out the treatment of like-kind exchange of investment real estate. These exchanges are a tool for deferring a potential tax bill at the sale of the property. IRC 1031 allows the sale proceeds to be moved into another investment real estate property/properties without triggering capital gains tax if done within the parameters spelled out by the IRS. There are a lot of specific rules around 1031 exchanges, so be sure to consult a tax professional, but if done correctly, this can be a great tool to allow the continued growth of the asset without losing a healthy chunk in the form of a tax bill.

Opportunity Zones: While investment real estate sales can use a 1031 exchange, real estate and other forms of capital gains that exist from selling a business, stocks, bonds, crypto-currency, or other assets, do not qualify for a 1031 exchange. Fortunately, by introducing Opportunity Zones, these types of capital gains can qualify for tax benefits.

Opportunity Zones are tax incentives designed to encourage those with capital gains to invest those gains into lower-income and undercapitalized communities. There are immense poten-tial financial benefits that are available through the Opportunity Zone legislation. These benefits include the deferral of the realization of the capital gain for a period and the permanent exclusion of new taxable gains if the investment is held for the allotted time. Currently, if investments are held for 10 years, an investor would pay no taxes on capital gains created through their investment in an Opportunity Zone Fund. In addition to the financial/tax benefits, there is the additional benefit of being a catalyst for improvement in undercapitalized areas. Again, make sure to consult your tax professional to make sure you are meet-ing the specific guidelines the IRS has outlined.

Retirement Plans: For business owners, you also have addi-tional potential tax levers to access through retirement plan structures. These could be 401(k)/solo 401(k)s, SEP IRAs, SIMPLE IRAs, Roth accounts, and pension accounts through a defined benefit or cash balance plan. Utilizing a self-directed custodian for these types of accounts allows for alternative assets to be held through some of these types of accounts. For those who are employees, you still have the ability to contribute to company retirement plans and make IRA or Roth IRA contributions within the IRS rules. Putting together the right investment account with the right assets can be a powerful combination for long-term results.

Legal Counsel: Besides having good tax advice, another key element is having access to legal counsel. One area for input would be the topic of Estate Planning. This team member can help you get legal documents that every person should have in place. This first set of documents would include a Will, which spells out your direct wishes for your property and assets, and if there are children involved, it spells out who you want to care for them. Please, parents, do this!

Additional documents that will be drafted as a part of your estate plan would be a power of attorney which appoints someone to manage your finances if you cannot do so yourself, and a healthcare directive which spells out care wishes and grants someone the authority to make medical decisions. Depending on your specific scenario, selling a Living Revocable Trust may also make sense. This trust would have specific purposes regarding holding assets or tax treatment. Is the trust's purpose avoiding assets passing through probate and paying probate taxes? Is there a special needs child for whom the trust is being set? Is the trust a tool for passing assets to subsequent generations in a tax-advantaged manner?

Asset protection is another area where a good attorney and insurance professional can be very helpful members of your team. As you accumulate more assets, there needs to be more thought put into how those are held and how to protect these from both a titling and insurance standpoint. Should these be held in your name individually, jointly with a spouse, or through an LLC or another entity? If a trust is established, what assets should be titled in the name of the trust?   A lifetime of hard work could be unwound by not giving this topic the proper amount of time.

Investment Design: I like to build an investment strategy similar to how I think about building a home. When you think of building a house, you only start putting up walls after you have a proper foundation. For your financial life, this foundation comes with having liquid funds for a rainy day.

Another piece of this foundation would be proper types of insurance. These insurances could include *homeowners' insurance, auto insurance, disability insurance, life insurance, renters' insurance, and liability coverages*. While this list is not exclusive, it gives you an idea of what protections are key to have in place.

As you move on placing investment dollars into an asset, as a starting point, I like to ask what is the purpose of the funds and when the funds will need to be accessed.   As you move outside the traditional financial markets, you can increase returns and stabilize values. Typically, these investments are tied to tangible assets, and the day-to-day volatility of the financial news cycle has a muted effect on these assets. What is typically lost in these is the ability to move these into cash quickly. This limitation is easily overcome by choosing different investments with different purposes. For example, I will put my long-term retirement money to work differently than those funds used for a home purchase in 24 months.

Knowing the impact of taxes on your investments and developing tax-efficient strategies can help you minimize taxes and maximize your returns.

It comes together when you set your mind on your Redefined American Dream and build wealth.

Understanding how your taxes work will help you break the "Money Shackles."

As an investor, you must be aware of the different types of taxes that can impact your investments, such as capital gains tax and dividend tax, and any associated penalty fees.

By knowing the tax implications of different investment options, you can make informed decisions that help you minimize taxes and maximize returns. You may encounter financial challenges like balancing short-term and long-term goals, but by developing strategies to overcome them, you can achieve your goals and build a successful investment portfolio towards creating your legacy and financial future.

Chapter Review

> If you'd like to practice what you've learned
> in this chapter, I invite you to check out the
> exercises at this link:
> https://therad.com/moneyshackles/workbook

The chapter exercises encourage you to analyze tax regulations and how they currently or will affect you, identify which regulations can protect your assets or eliminate taxes, and strategize which ones can feasibly support you now and plan how to utilize other codes in the future.

1. It's important to understand *Tax Codes and Regulations* like capital gains tax and dividend tax, and stay informed of changes to achieve financial goals through investments. Seek professional help to limit tax exposure and maximize returns, and don't forget to prioritize financial education to achieve long-term financial freedom.

2. Achieving financial freedom with the *Tax Circle* requires utilizing tax shelters and building a diverse team of experts, including tax strategists and legal counsel, to develop tax-efficient investment strategies and ensure proper asset protection. Financial education is key to making informed investment decisions and maximizing returns, so don't hesitate to seek professional help and stay informed of changes in regulations and tax codes.

3. Maximizing returns and reducing tax liabilities can be achieved through a *Tax Strategy*, such as 1031 Exchanges, Opportunity Zones, retirement plans, legal counsel for estate planning and asset protection, and investment design.

Utilize these strategies to defer or eliminate taxes on capital gains, take advantage of tax benefits for business owners, and protect your assets through estate planning and proper investment design.

What are the tips for choosing the right team? Why do taxes matter in achieving your Redefined American Dream? Tips for choosing the right team to achieve your financial goals require prioritizing experts in tax strategies and legal counsel for asset protection and estate planning. Taxes matter because understanding tax regulations and utilizing tax strategies can help defer or eliminate taxes on capital gains, take advantage of tax benefits for business owners, and protect your assets.

CHAPTER 10

BUILDING YOUR LEGACY AND MAKING A POSITIVE IMPACT

How do you align your wealth-building education with your legacy and dreams?

Money can certainly enhance certain aspects of life, but it's not a guaranteed source of happiness. Your level of joy and contentment doesn't automatically increase with your bank account balance. There's a flip side to the coin. If you're already feeling empty or unhappy, having more money won't fix that. For me, I've discovered that finding purpose and meaning in my actions is what brings me true fulfillment. That's what legacy is all about.

Building a legacy is about more than just accumulating wealth or assets. It's about creating a lasting impact beyond your lifetime and positively affecting future generations. By investing in wealth-building education, you can develop the knowledge and skills necessary to make sound financial decisions that will enable you to achieve your legacy goals.

My original legacy was making sure my sons would never suffer the way I did growing up. The money I made gave me the sense they could choose their life path without the concern of money. I have come to realize that the real legacy I'm building with my sons, my family, and my Tribe is an everlasting legacy of knowledge, values, and a joyous pursuit of their passions. We will continuously give back and make an impact for generations. Shifting generational curses while changing how our country views money. Ending the "Money Shackles" while changing the American conversation about money.

I've found a sense of purpose in various ways throughout my life. From building and creating things with my business to positively impacting people's lives and, of course, with my family and friendships. Building a legacy is crucial - leaving something behind for your children and future generations that improve the world.

Defining what legacy means to you is also an essential part of the process. Consider the impact you want to make on your family, community, and the world. Think about the values that you want to be associated with and the causes that are important to you. By clarifying your legacy goals, you can make more intentional and impactful decisions about allocating your resources and building a lasting legacy.

It's a key part of the American Dream to want to give your children a better life than you had.

As parents, we all want to provide the best possible future for our children. One way to do that is by teaching them the basics of investing and financial literacy. In today's increasingly complex world, **Educating Children** at an early stage on their journey as successful investors and confident individuals is more important than ever.

So, how do we help kids of all ages achieve financial freedom and make their dreams come true? It all starts with incorporating little financial lessons into our everyday conversations. Using games to teach kids how to save, the importance of investing, and the consequences of poor financial decision-making. We can make a real difference in their journey by constantly reminding them of their goals and having weekly discussions to keep them focused. Consider the following:

- Allowance management and teach your child how to manage saving, spending, and giving.

- Practice delayed gratification and set savings goals if there's something your child really wants to buy.

- Get your children involved in financial decisions, such as choosing a grocery store and comparing prices of items, or even in the process of your financial plans, like debt management, investment education, and tax strategies.

- Create a budget with money buckets and teach your child how to make money work through income, living costs, and investing.

- If your child is slightly older, teach them money personalities and how they change over time, and train them to utilize their strengths and weaknesses.

As your children grow older, continuing their financial education is vital.

Help prepare them for the future by teaching them about finance, including how it can help them save money and use compounding strategies to achieve their goals. Cover topics such as interest, credit, taxes, and regulations, giving them the tools to navigate the financial world. Introduce the idea of alternative investments to diversify their portfolio and stress the importance of due diligence in making informed financial decisions. By guiding them through the Financial Decision Tree, you empower them to make wise choices that shape their future.

Building a continuous legacy requires wealth-building education as early as possible, so future generations can also begin making informed financial decisions that align with their long-term goals and values.

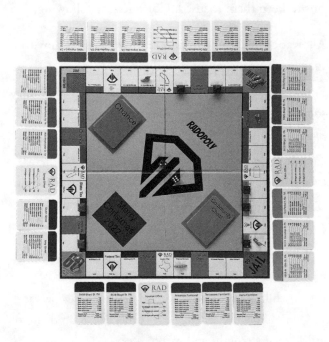

At the end of the day, leaving a legacy means having a lasting impact on the world.

Legacy is about doing something that matters beyond yourself. It's what brings true meaning to our lives.

Proper planning and financial management are critical components of building a legacy. By setting clear goals and developing a comprehensive financial plan, you can ensure that your resources are being allocated in ways that align with your values and priorities. This may involve creating a charitable foundation, establishing a trust or endowment, or investing in businesses or initiatives that align with your values and contribute to your legacy.

The ultimate goal of building a legacy is to positively impact the world and leave a lasting reflection of your values and priorities. To achieve this, you can invest in wealth-building education, develop a comprehensive financial plan, and define your legacy goals. This approach enables you to create a legacy that extends beyond your lifetime and positively impacts future generations.

Building and preserving wealth requires a comprehensive approach that includes long-term investment strategies and effective estate planning.

One key strategy for building wealth is to invest in options that offer long-term growth and stability. This might include investments in stocks, real estate, or other assets with a history of strong returns and consistent growth. Also, establishing trusts and other vehicles can help preserve and transfer wealth to future generations, ensuring that your legacy continues to grow and thrive over time.

Another essential component of building and ensuring your legacy is effective estate planning. This involves understanding the legal and financial implications of estate planning, identifying potential roadblocks, and avoiding them. For example, creating a will, establishing a trust, and designating beneficiaries for your retirement accounts can all help to ensure that your assets are distributed according to your wishes and that your legacy is protected for future generations.

It's also important to regularly review and update your estate plan to ensure it remains relevant and reflects any changes in your financial situation or family circumstances. This might include updating beneficiary designations, changing your will or trust, or adjusting your investment strategies to reflect market changes or priorities.

Building and ensuring your legacy requires a long-term approach incorporating wealth-building strategies and effective estate planning. By investing in options that offer long-term growth and stability, establishing trusts and other vehicles to preserve and transfer wealth, and ensuring that your estate plan remains relevant and up-to-date, you can create a lasting legacy reflecting your values and priorities for future generations.

Legacy is more than just physical possessions and legacies. It's about your impact on people's lives and how they remember you. When it comes to money, it's important to start having conversations about our relationship with it early on. Most people aren't even aware of their money mindset and how it affects their financial decisions.

It's no secret that upbringing plays a big role in shaping our beliefs and behaviors around money. As children, we learn from our parents and the dynamics we observe within our family.

What we learned from our parents about money can have a lasting impact on how we handle our finances in adulthood, and it's not always positive. Many people feel like they're "messed up" about money, often because of how they were taught about it as kids.

The good news is that acknowledging this is the first step to making a change. If you're willing to recognize how your past experiences with money have shaped your current mindset, you're already on the path to improving your relationship with finances. If you're serious about leaving a legacy or making a positive impact, it's important to embark on a personal journey of growth and self-discovery.

Ultimately, it's not just about the money. It's about living an incredible life and passing that on to others. When you focus on that, financial success will follow.

Educating your children and grandchildren about financial management is critical for leaving a lasting impact and ensuring that your legacy continues responsibly and sustainably.

However, that alone doesn't give my life meaning. My family, my children, and my friendships are the things that give me a greater purpose and meaning. Legacy is important to me.

One way to accomplish this is by having open and honest conversations about money with your children from an early age.

Our Tribe members Robin and Jeff Thomas emphasize teaching financial literacy and building a legacy. Robin says, "I want to build a legacy for my grandchildren and teach them about financial literacy. I'm hiring them in my businesses so I can start Roth IRAs for them. I want to show them how their money can grow over time and help them build a strong financial foundation for their future. It's exciting to see their eyes light up when they see the potential growth of their investments."

By teaching children about basic financial concepts such as budgeting, saving, and investing, parents can help set their children up for long-term financial success. This understanding can lead to smart financial decision-making, including long-term investing and compound interest benefits. One of my favorites is when my 6-year-old gives me money and says, "Dad, buy another house."

Instilling a strong foundation of financial literacy and utilizing smart investment options can help set up children and grandchildren for long-term financial success and security. However, achieving this goal requires a multifaceted approach.

On the one hand, it's important to provide children and grandchildren with financial education early. This can include teaching them budgeting, saving, investing, and other key financial concepts. Parents and grandparents can also encourage financial literacy by giving them access to educational resources, such as books, videos, and games.

On the other hand, leading by example is an effective strategy for imparting financial education. Modeling responsible financial behavior, such as living within your means, prioritizing saving and investing, and avoiding debt, can help reinforce good financial habits and attitudes in your children and grandchildren. Additionally, involving them in financial discussions and decision-making can help build their confidence and skills in managing their finances.

By combining education, modeling, and active involvement, parents and grandparents can help set up the next generation for long-term financial success and security. It takes effort, patience, and consistency, but the benefits are worth it.

As part of your estate planning, you might also consider setting up trusts or other vehicles that can help support future generations' financial education. For example, establishing a trust that requires beneficiaries to complete financial education courses or meet certain financial goals before accessing funds can help to promote responsible financial behavior and ensure that your legacy is carried on responsibly and sustainably.

Leaving a legacy through financial education requires a long-term approach emphasizing financial literacy and responsible financial behavior. By starting early, leading by example, and incorporating financial education into your **Estate Planning**, you can ensure that your legacy is carried responsibly and sustainably for future generations.

Retirement Planning is essential for long-term financial security, and understanding the different retirement savings options available can help you maximize your savings and minimize your tax burden.

One common retirement savings option is the 401(k), which many employers offer as a way for their employees to save for retirement. Contributions to a 401(k) are tax-deductible, and many employers also offer matching contributions, which can help to boost your savings even further. Another popular retirement savings option is the Individual Retirement Account (IRA), which offers tax-deferred growth and a range of investment options. One important detail to remember is that there are contribution limits for 401(k)s and IRAs. As of 2022, the contribution limit for a 401(k) is $20,500 per year for those under 50 years old and $27,000 for those 50 and over. The contribution limit for an IRA is $6,000 per year for those under 50 years old and $7,000 for those 50 and over. It's also worth noting that there are different types of IRAs, including traditional and Roth, each with unique tax benefits and eligibility requirements. Researching and consulting a financial advisor is important to determine which retirement savings options are best for your financial situation and goals.

When it comes to retirement savings, understanding the benefits and drawbacks of each plan is key to making informed decisions. Maximizing contributions is also important, which may mean contributing the maximum allowed each year, taking advantage of employer matches, and regularly reviewing investment options to ensure they align with long-term financial goals.

Taking retirement a step further is estate planning. To ensure that your wealth is protected and passed to future generations correctly, estate planning is essential.

Proper estate planning includes many documents: a will and a living will, a living revocable trust, a power attorney, and a health care surrogacy. These documents are essential to estate planning because they allow you to control how your legacy lives beyond you and ensure it passes appropriately to the people you wish to continue it. It avoids probate, the public court process in which your legacy will be distributed based on the court's opinion. An opinion that may not align with how you want your assets and wealth handled.

- A will allows you to clearly state how you wish to distribute assets and wealth or who you want to manage these things upon your death.

- A living will gives you the same ability to control the management of your legacy in the case of incapacitation while you're still living.

- A livable revocable trust will allow you to identify a trustee for your wealth, designate beneficiaries of your legacy, transfer assets, and establish terms on how your wealth is managed after you're gone.

- Power of attorney allows you to appoint someone to manage your assets and wealth while defining their scope of authority and duration of management if you have young children who are the primary beneficiaries of your legacy but are not ready to manage it.

- Health care surrogacy (aka medical proxy, or advance healthcare directive) is designating a decision-maker for your medical treatment if you cannot. You can specify the scope in which the surrogate can make decisions, whether broad or limited, and you can include specific wishes for handling your physical being after your time has come.

Not only do these documents help you clearly state how you wish your legacy to be distributed and managed, but it also protects your assets from the state and gives you more control of the direction your legacy lives and grows based on your true wishes.

Beyond financial, retirement, and estate planning, it's important to consider ways to give back and positively impact your community, not just during retirement or death. Every person, with their unique destiny, will have an equally unique legacy to leave for future generations. You may not realize it, but you WILL leave a legacy. The question is not if but how.

Your specific impact through **Legacy Planning** will consist of a financial inheritance and many other influences based on your habits, role modeling, teaching, giving, and heart. These facets reflect what is important to you during your life and will continue to show up in your lasting impact after you are gone. Even those who think, "I have nothing," can leave a trail of good – or bad – habits, teachings, and other actions that influence the next generation. You may think foolishly you can conscientiously choose to not leave a legacy. However, the sooner you realize that your impact is inevitable, the sooner you can begin to act toward investing—and compounding —the impact you *want to* leave rather than risking leaving one you don't want.

Start here. Wealth is on your mind now. What financial habits do you want your children and grandchildren to practice? Begin practicing them now. The knowledge and wisdom prioritize your time for those conversations. Now, do the same with your greater legacy. What values do you want to instill? You may have spiritual principles and practices, civic responsibilities and duties of citizenship, wisdom for marriage and parenting, or demonstrations of humanitarianism.

Your habits and knowledge are supported (and multiplied) by partnering with organizations dedicated to the same mission. Volunteering, donating to charity, and supporting causes you care about can provide a sense of purpose and fulfillment in retirement while making a difference in the world.

To achieve retirement and leave a legacy for our children, we must take a long-term approach, prioritizing financial security and personal fulfillment. This means understanding retirement savings options, maximizing contributions, and finding ways to give back in retirement. Doing so can extend our Real American Dream beyond our working years and positively impact future generations.

Combining financial planning with a sense of purpose and meaning can create a retirement that reflects our values and leaves a legacy of positive impact. Building a legacy isn't just about accumulating wealth. It's about creating a sense of purpose and tradition that we can pass down. There are many ways to achieve this, such as investing in real estate or living purpose-driven lives.

The ultimate key to leaving a meaningful legacy is to prioritize our values, whether it's through philanthropy, community involvement, or passing on our knowledge and skills to the next generation. Doing so can create a ripple effect of a positive impact extending beyond our lifetime. It takes planning and effort, but the rewards of building a legacy are immeasurable for us and future generations.

One key aspect of building a strong legacy is instilling financial literacy in our children. By teaching them how to make smart financial decisions and setting them up for long-term success, we can help create a solid financial foundation that will benefit future generations.

It's not just about investing in financial assets. Our investment decisions, whatever they may be, can contribute to the legacy we leave behind.

Ultimately, the legacy we leave reflects who we are and what we stand for. By focusing on building a legacy that our children and grandchildren can be proud of, we can create positive impacts that will last for generations. Whether through financial planning or other means, investing in our future is one of the most meaningful gifts we can give to the people we love. We can begin to build a legacy that will inspire and enrich the lives of those who come after us.

Chapter Review

> If you'd like to practice what you've learned in this chapter, I invite you to check out the exercises at this link:
> https://therad.com/moneyshackles/workbook

The chapter exercises encourage you to discuss different tactics to educate family members, including children or grandchildren, identify the key components of estate planning and why it is important to transfer wealth, and understand the importance of a personal journey of growth and self-discovery to make an impact with your newfound financial freedom.

1. *Educating Children* about investing and financial literacy is essential for securing their future success. In today's complex world, giving your children an early start on their journey to becoming confident, knowledgeable investor is a powerful tool for building generational wealth and securing your family's legacy.

2. *Estate Planning* involves proper retirement planning and financial management, and the key strategy is to invest in options that offer long-term growth and stability. Estate planning is also essential to protect and transfer wealth to future generations.

3. *Legacy Planning* goes beyond physical possessions. It involves a lasting impact on the world, and the ultimate goal is to positively impact the world by leaving a lasting reflection of your values and priorities. A personal journey of growth and self-discovery is important to find purpose in your life's work and leave a legacy.

How do you align your wealth-building education with your legacy and dreams? Aligning your wealth-building education with your legacy and dreams involves teaching your children about financial literacy and investing for generational wealth, proper retirement planning through long-term investments, and estate planning to protect and transfer wealth. However, legacy planning also involves a personal journey of growth and self-discovery to leave a lasting impact on the world by reflecting on your values and priorities.

CHAPTER 11

UNLOCKING YOUR FINANCIAL POTENTIAL

How can you finally overcome your "Money Shackles" and take control of your future?

What I've come to realize is that success isn't a stroke of luck.

He was a man on a mission. I first met Eric Snell on a buying trip after he joined RAD Diversified. I remember him saying, "I realized that if I wanted to change my financial future, I needed to take control of my own destiny and learn everything I could about personal finance."

He identified his financial goals and developed a plan to achieve them. It wasn't some vague idea of "getting rich." Eric had a clear vision of what he wanted his future to look like, and he took massive action to make it a reality: "It's about being able to invest enough that the returns from the investment can free me from the nine to five."

Who doesn't want that? It's about having the security and mobility of financial freedom. The dream is to be free from the chains of the daily grind and retire comfortably or pursue your purpose.

The reality is most people feel trapped and uncertain about their financial future. They're stuck.

Are you stuck? Are you tired and feeling uncertain about your financial future? Whether at the beginning or middle of your financial journey, you might be unsure about what steps to take to move progressively forward to break free of the wealth gap.

The Redefined American Dream isn't out of reach.

As you begin the journey toward unlocking your financial potential, you may feel weighed down by what may seem like insurmountable barriers to achieving financial freedom. These "Money Shackles" could be anything from debt to a lack of investment opportunities or a scarcity mindset. You should've realized that these **Overcoming Barriers** with the right mindset and strategies is possible.

It's all about breaking out from the "Freedom Trap" and finding your sense of financial purpose. With the right mindset, strategy, and guidance, you can become a good investor and eventually break the "Money Shackles" to become a great investor and achieve true financial freedom.

You have to ask yourself, are you ready? Are you ready to take control and unlock your financial potential?

It's time to stop dreaming and start doing.

One strategy to overcome these barriers is an investment mindset, greater education, and wise action. Align yourself with the right organizations with strong leadership and avoid the pitfalls of mainstream media propaganda.

Eric's commitment to learning created major changes in his life. He was willing to do what it took, even when initially skeptical of the process. He learned:

- The importance of assessing his current financial situation and determining where he wanted it to go,

- How his relationship with money could help him by managing his investment risks in money buckets,

- The power of money working for him through borrowing and compound interest,

- Building a diversified investment portfolio with alternative investments and real estate,

- How becoming a Fractional Owner frees up his time to live a balanced life,

- Navigating tax codes and regulations with the right team, and

- Adjusting his financial plan regularly to stay on track as his dreams change to create a lasting legacy and impact.

Ultimately, taking control of your financial destiny is about making choices and decisions that empower you to live the life of your dreams. It may involve alternative investments, diversification, and even taxation strategies. It is a never-ending pursuit to become healthier in your relationship with money and to take action to access better financial opportunities.

Eric's story is a reminder that achieving financial freedom is possible, even for those who struggle to understand complex financial concepts. It requires dedication, hard work, and a willingness to continually learn and grow. The reward is well worth the effort.

Perhaps the most inspiring aspect of Eric's journey was his ability to stay motivated and committed to his financial goals, even when things got tough. He developed a positive mindset and attitude towards money, celebrated small successes and milestones, and surrounded himself with like-minded individuals who supported and encouraged him.

I can't highlight that point enough. A supportive network is necessary to help you build wealth.

"There's that saying that if you want to go fast, go alone. And if you want to go far, go together….RADD is kind of the exception to that. RADD is moving faster than I can. There are so many new investments and so many new things going on with RADD. I can't even keep up with everything that's going on, but you can tell that it's being built for long-term stability. So I think RADD is an exception to that rule, going fast and far [together]."

What does a life without "Money Shackles" look like?

It's about taking control of your life and money instead of vice versa. It's about living the American Dream on your own terms and leaving a legacy for future generations to fulfill their purpose and dreams.

I believe that by sharing Eric's story and teaching these valuable lessons, I can help you develop a similar mindset and approach toward your financial goals. By taking the time to learn about personal finance, investing, and wealth creation, Eric was able to make informed decisions that helped him grow his wealth over time. In addition, he avoided common pitfalls and mistakes that could derail even the most well-intentioned financial plans. By teaching these lessons, I hope to empower you with the knowledge and tools to become financially literate and achieve your goals of Redefining your American Dream.

You've got the basics down. Now it's time to level up your financial education and achieve even greater success.

Look at the growing Decision Tree Matrix. It started as a sapling in Chapter 2 by defining important interests to maintain a healthy balance in life and financial planning. Then grew strong enough to offer shade as investment options expanded earning potential to appreciate capital in Chapter 6. Now, it's producing fruit to take the journey further.

As you continue to grow your Decision Tree Matrix with your actions, you'll see the difference between being a good investor and a great one. A good investor finds decent opportunities and makes a return on their investment. In contrast, great investors realize everything they need to do to invest using leverage to make as much money as possible.

By mastering these concepts and advancing your investment strategies, you will be well on your way to achieving your financial goals and taking control of your future. It's not just about technical knowledge and skills—it's also about embracing your financial future with confidence and optimism.

By implementing the lessons and principles in this book, you have already set yourself apart from the average investor. But what if you could do even more?

What if you could not only achieve your financial goals but also positively impact society as a whole?

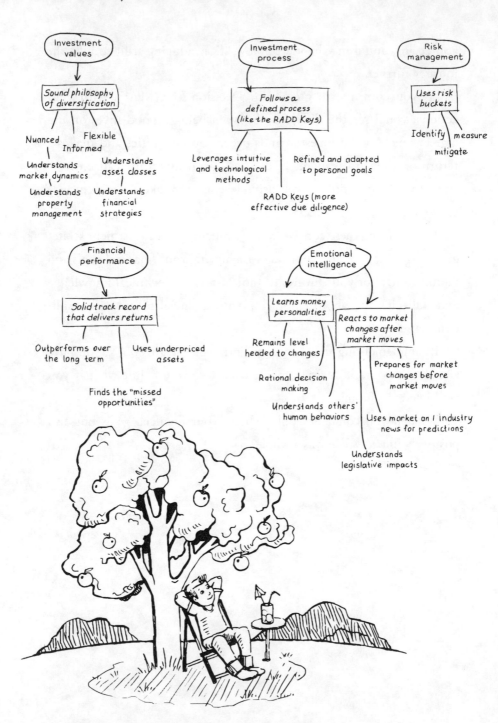

Investment values → Sound philosophy of diversification

Nuanced
Flexible
Informed
Understands market dynamics
Understands asset classes
Understands property management
Understands financial strategies

Investment process → Follows a defined process (like the RADD Keys)

Leverages intuitive and technological methods
Refined and adapted to personal goals
RADD Keys (more effective due diligence)

Risk management → Uses risk buckets

Identify   measure
mitigate

Financial performance → Solid track record that delivers returns

Outperforms over the long term
Uses underpriced assets
Finds the "missed opportunities"

Emotional intelligence → Learns money personalities / Reacts to market changes after market moves

Remains level headed to changes
Rational decision making
Understands others' human behaviors

Prepares for market changes before market moves
Uses market an I industry news for predictions
Understands legislative impacts

A great investor can live sustainably with only their investments

This is where becoming a **Great Investor** comes into play. A great investor makes smart investment decisions, understands the market, and makes decisions before it moves. They realize that:

- Committing to continuous education is essential for staying updated with the evolving investing world.

- Creating a balanced and diversified portfolio minimizes risks and maximizes potential returns.

- Taking calculated risks involves strategic analysis to make informed decisions with the potential for significant gains.

- Developing a long-term perspective avoids getting caught up in short-term fluctuations and aligns with goals.

- Staying disciplined and patient, following investment plans, helps weather market volatility and achieve long-term success.

By doing so, great investors benefit themselves and contribute to society by supporting stable economies and stronger businesses. You have the power to be a great investor and make a lasting impact on the world. So take what you have learned and keep striving for greatness.

Help me help you change the game.

This isn't just a financial playbook. It's the financial movement of our lifetime.

What if everyone had access to this knowledge? Imagine a world where people are financially educated and confident in managing their money. It would not only benefit them individually, but collectively it would also impact society as a whole.

It takes a **Financial Movement** to make that change.

With society's better understanding of their financial situation and goals, individuals could make informed decisions that align with their values and priorities. They could invest in their future and contribute to their communities meaningfully. A financially literate society could lead to more stable economies, stronger businesses, and a better quality of life for everyone.

History is filled with change makers, like Harriet Tubman, Thomas Edison, Orville and Wilbur Wright, Albert Einstein, and Dr. Martin Luther King, Jr.

They made history not by sitting around watching but by taking action.[38]

Dr. King is remembered for his famous "I Have a Dream" speech, delivered on Aug. 28, 1963 at the Lincoln Memorial in Washington D.C. He believed that each individual has agency and power. His passion for that change and his powerful ability to communicate a message that mattered impacted millions.[39] "I believe" impacts every life in this country.

Agency and power.

Dr. King's and many other Civil Rights activists' transformative work in the Civil Rights Movement and the subsequent dismantling of discriminatory practices in education and employment played a significant role[40] in the growth of the middle-class,[41] allowing America to become more competitive in the global economy.

38   King Jr., ML. 1964. *Why We Can't Wait.* Harper & Row.

39   Shelby, T and Terry, BM. 2018. T*o Shape a New World: Essays on the Political Philosophy of Martin Luther King, Jr.* Harvard University Press.

40   Ryssdal, K and Cunningham, R. 2023. *Understanding the civil rights movement as a labor and economic movement.* Retrieved from https://www.marketplace.org/2023/02/23/understanding-the-civil-rights-movement-as-a-labor-and-economic-movement/.

41   Bayer, P and Charles, KK. 2016 (2017). *Divergent Paths: Structural Change, Economic Rank, and the Evolution of Black-White Earnings Differences, 1940-2014.* Retrieved from https://www.nber.org/papers/w22797.

Yet, this wasn't the only movement to affect economic growth throughout history.

My Dream is to help you break free of the systematic "Money Shackles" and end the inequality of opportunity in America. It's time to take back your American Dream and regain your right to FREEDOM. —Dutch Mendenhall

We could do the same in America with each individual's personal agency and power.

Take decisive actionable steps in your financial journey.

Remember, this is not the end—it's just the beginning.

Wake up every day and ask yourself these two questions:

If not now…when? If not me…who?

Chapter Review

> If you'd like to practice what you've learned in this chapter, I invite you to check out the exercises at this link:
> https://therad.com/moneyshackles/workbook

The chapter exercises encourage you to evaluate how you will continuously grow and develop despite potential barriers while remaining true to your journey, establish further steps to become a great investor with the Financial Decision Tree, and look at the accumulation of all of the information you have gained to act on your new financial plan to your Redefined American Dream.

1. Achieving financial freedom is possible when ***Overcoming Barriers***. With the right mindset, strategy, and guidance, and it's about taking control of your life and your money instead of the other way around to live the American Dream on your own terms and leave a legacy for future generations.

2. Use the Financial Decision Tree to become a ***Great Investor***. By desiring to positively impact society, you can continue to grow your Financial Decision Tree, create continuous education, have a balanced and diversified portfolio, take calculated risks, develop a long-term perspective, and stay disciplined and patient to achieve long-term success.

3. You have the power and agency to create a ***Financial Movement*** that positively impacts society by educating yourself, taking control of your finances,

advocating for change, and engaging with others to create a supportive environment.

How can you finally overcome your "Money Shackles" and take control of your future? To finally overcome your "Money Shackles" and take control of your future, you must develop a clear vision of your financial goals, create a plan to achieve them, enhance innovation and growth in your investments and mindset, become a good investor, and have the dedication, hard work, and a willingness to continually learn and grow.

WORDS TO KNOW

The power you have in your journey toward financial freedom should not be underestimated. It will be your fuel to keep you going when things get tough. It will allow you to look beyond the "Freedom Traps" you may face and believe in a better future by breaking free from your "Money Shackles". With this power, you will actively pursue your goals, choosing them over the status quo, even when progress seems slow. Without confidence in your new path, giving up on your dreams and settling for less than what you deserve is easy. Be brave and allow the embers of your ambition to blaze into flames as you navigate the ups and downs of your financial journey. Hold onto these lessons and let them guide you toward a brighter and more abundant future.

Alternative Investments are innovative opportunities often outside traditional stock and bond marketplaces. It's important to note that these investment vehicles come with increased risk but also have the potential for higher returns. Risk comes from not knowing what you're doing, so educating yourself on the potential risks and rewards is essential before jumping into alternative investments.

Diversification is an investment strategy that reduces risk by allocating investments across various asset classes, industries, and geographies. Three buckets to consider are low, moderate, and high-risk investments. *Fractional Ownership* is a powerful strategy that allows you to invest in all three of these buckets. Examples of Fractional Ownership can include but are not limited to partial ownership of a business, housing, or farm. This approach can help balance the risks and rewards, helping to protect investments during volatile markets while also taking advantage of opportunities that arise.

Freedom Traps are created by the conventional system that, rather than giving freedom, limits people's ability to achieve real wealth. It allows barriers to entry that can include a lack of access to resources and information, as well as the difficulty of breaking free from societal and cultural norms that reinforce these "Freedom Traps." Examples include societal peer pressures, political propaganda, biased media, and the lack of financial education provided by institutional systems. This system prevents individuals from breaking free from their "Money Shackles." These "Freedom Traps" create a vicious cycle that keeps individuals from achieving their financial goals and realizing their version of the American Dream. Overcoming these barriers and breaking free from "Freedom Traps" requires education, awareness, and a willingness to challenge societal norms and think outside the box.

Money Shackles are financial obligations and self-imposed limitations that can disable individuals' financial freedom. As Warren Buffet said, "The chains of habit are too light to be felt until they are too heavy to be broken."[1] Breaking free from "Money Shackles" requires taking control of your financial situation, making smart alternative decisions, making money and debt work for you, and investing in your future.

Redefined American Dream is your ability to create financial freedom, a lifestyle that you choose to live, and craft a purpose-driven legacy and impact. It is achieved by finding new investment opportunities that

---

1   From: Buffett, Warren, and Lawrence A. Cunningham. 1998, "The Essays of Warren Buffett: Lessons for Corporate America." The Cunningham Group.

align with your values and goals. The traditional American Dream of homeownership, a white picket fence, and retirement with a decent stock portfolio are no longer feasible for many people. Embracing the Redefined American Dream requires a mindset shift and a commitment to taking bold action toward your financial goals.

ABOUT THE AUTHOR
AND TheRAD™

DUTCH MENDENHALL IS THE FOUNDER of RAD Diversified (RADD), President of the Alternate Investment Association (AIA), and the recipient of the Patriot Award for his work with Veterans. He is a pioneer of innovation and growth within the American Dream. With over 15 years of experience in real estate and education, Mendenhall has demonstrated his expertise and authority as a "Thought Leader" in the industry. Moreover, his personal experiences have contributed to his success, as reflected in his work with RAD Diversified.

TheRAD™, the educational entity, addresses crucial issues such as empowering individuals to Redefine their American Dream through smart investing and diversification. It is designed for anyone seeking to leverage their wealth to create positive social change and achieve financial freedom. The program aims to empower individuals and families to secure a prosperous future through the strength of real estate investments done right and done together. Whether someone is looking to improve their financial situation, struggling with debt, or interested in alternative investment methods and diversification strategies, TheRAD is the gateway to a better future.

Dutch Mendenhall and his team thrive on facing the challenges in today's society and market. They aim to make a difference in people's lives, so they prioritize taking action and educating themselves on various industries and investment strategies that keep them ahead as market leaders. They make informed decisions and transform their lifestyle to continue putting them in positions to succeed. This approach has helped them build TheRAD™ brand, which thrives and serves the community of investors they work with and care about.

For Mendenhall and his team, empowering others with financial knowledge and creating a community of like-minded individuals who support each other's goals is crucial. They believe in fostering strong relationships based on trust, transparency, and accountability. This approach has helped them build a Tribe invested in each other's success.

Their dedication to education, community-building, and transformative investment strategies sets Mendenhall and his team apart. Their commitment to positively impacting people's lives and creating a legacy of financial empowerment for future generations is unprecedented in today's wealth-building environment. Their philosophy proves to be a separator between them and the rest of the industry.

When analyzing the meaning of the American Dream from history to the present day, it becomes clear that innovation and growth are key factors in achieving success. Dutch Mendenhall has the knowledge and skills to address these issues and jump-start a revolutionary financial movement. His approach has been proven effective through case studies and real-world examples.

Implementing Mendenhall's solutions involves putting the relevant lessons learned to the test against traditional thinking and powerful economic waves. With his expertise and that of his team, they have the ability to make an impact on the industry never seen before. Mendenhall's approach prioritizes financial education, community building, and transformative investment strategies that empower investors to break free from financial limitations and achieve their goals.

Beyond market leadership and financial empowerment, Mendenhall firmly believes in giving back to the communities and efforts that lift us and make the world a better place. That's why he is one of the biggest supporters and contributors to two outstanding Veteran support organizations, Special Operations Wounded Warrior and Task Force Dagger. They are dedicated to helping our Veterans and their families overcome the challenges our heroes face in their day-to-day life after service. Mendenhall is also a supporter of Aerial and Joshua House. Aerial, a global humanitarian organization responding to natural disasters and combat trafficking with the help of first responders and Veterans. Joshua House, a safe haven for abused and neglected children.

Overall, TheRAD™ team's dedication to innovation, growth, expertise, and experience make them a viable option for those looking to achieve financial success and transform their lives. Their practical and effective solutions make them a valuable resource for anyone looking to break free from financial limitations and achieve their idea of the American Dream.

Redefining the American Dream with new mindsets and leveraging traditional values can lead to success. This book explores the impact of implementing the tips, techniques, and lessons learned from this book. It will give you the tools to create the plan that turns your life into your American Dream.

Dutch Mendenhall and TheRAD lead the way toward a brighter future for all Americans. Addressing the wealth crisis and promoting innovation and growth paved the way for everyone to unlock their vision for their future. The story is not over, but together, we can achieve the new American Dream with the right mindset and actions.

WEBSITES

RAD Diversified REIT
(https://raddiversified.com/)

RADD Inner Circle
(https://icradd.com/)

RADD America
(https://raddamerica.com/)

TheRAD
(https://therad.com/)

The RADD Podcast
(https://www.theraddpodcast.com/)